Malawi Mailings

© Copyright 2014 Rodney and Sarah Schofield

All rights reserved. No part of this publication may be reproduced, stored in a retrieval system, or transmltted in any form or by any means, electronic, mechanical, photocopying, recording or otherwise, without prior permission from the publishers.

Published by

Mzuni Press
P/Bag 201
Luwinga, Mzuzu 2, Malawi

ISBN 978-99908-0246-7 (Mzuni Press)

Mzuni Press is represented outside Africa by:
African Books Collective Oxford (also for e-books)
(orders@africanbookscollective.com)

www.mzunipress.luviri.net
www.africanbookscollective.com

Malawi Mailings

Reflections on Missionary Life 2000 – 2003

Rodney and Sarah Schofield

Mzuni Press 2014

*Dedicated to the memory of Fr Rodney Hunter,
'missionary, pastor and friend to the people of Malawi'.*

Previously published titles by Rodney Schofield

Jubilee Reflections:
    Rich and Poor in Christian Perspective (2001)
Mystery or Magic:
    Biblical Replies to the Heterodox (2004)
Bordering on Faith:
    Developing Orthopraxis in Response to Spiritual Need (2009)
The Emerging Church:
    Christian Communities in the Earliest Times (2012)

Acknowledgements

We are very grateful to friends in Zomba from whom we learnt so much about the country, especially Stephen Carr and John Wilson.

We were also given many insights into African religion during our preparation at Selly Oak, Birmingham by both Patrick Kalilombe and Allan Anderson.

Thanks go as well to many friends and parishes in England who supported us during our four years in Malawi, and to whom these monthly reports were sent.

Rodney and Sarah Schofield
served as missionaries
with the United Society for the Propagation of the Gospel
in Zomba, Malawi, Central Africa from 2000 to 2003.

Rodney, who prepared the text with Sarah's help, taught at the ecumenical
Zomba Theological College (ZTC)
and for a time was also parish priest of St George's Anglican Church.

Sarah, who drew the illustrations, was involved with orphan care in their
home and in Songani Community Care Group
as well as teaching English and crafts at ZTC.

*Their previous experience in Africa was in Lesotho from 1984 to 1986
when Rodney was Warden of Lelapa la Jesu Seminary in Roma.*

CONTENTS

Introduction
Page 1
Partnership in Faith – First Impressions

Year 2000
Page 11
Drinking in the Atmosphere – An Overview of Theological Training
The Common Good – Breaking the Silence – Jubilee South – Faith in the Future
A Clash of Cultures – Protective Magic – African Christianity
Language of the Heart – Challenges and Constraints – Putting Down Roots

Year 2001
Page 59
The Role of Repetition – Looking Ahead – Life in the Raw – Proverbial Sayings
Out and About – A Week in the Diary – The Impact of AIDS – The Response to AIDS
New Developments – Orphan Support – The Need for Reparation
The Ethical Dimension of Community

Year 2002
Page 103
Witchcraft Beliefs – Contemplation and Struggle – The Maize Crisis – Child Labour
A New Diocese – Poverty Issues – Africans Abroad – Veneration of Ancestors
Fishing Tactics – The Hunger Months Resume – Coming Soon
Seasonal Meditations

Year 2003
Page 143
Resilience and Joy – An Interregnum – The Anglican Heartland
Provincial Autonomy – Power Crisis – Our New Bishop – The Process of Formation
A Beautiful Country – Ntiya News – Links and Plans

Postscript
Page 181
Poinsettia

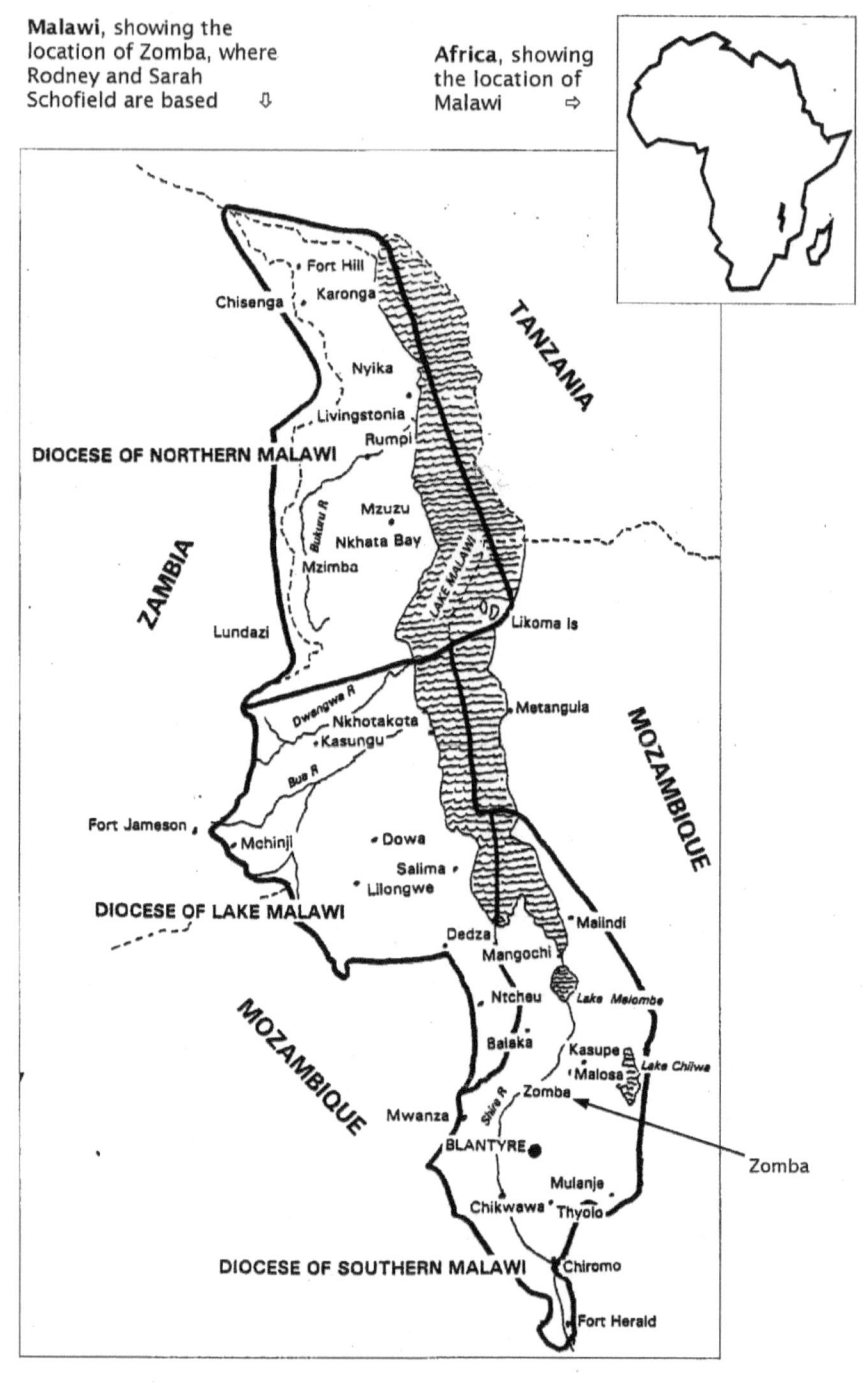

Malawi, showing the location of Zomba, where Rodney and Sarah Schofield are based

Africa, showing the location of Malawi

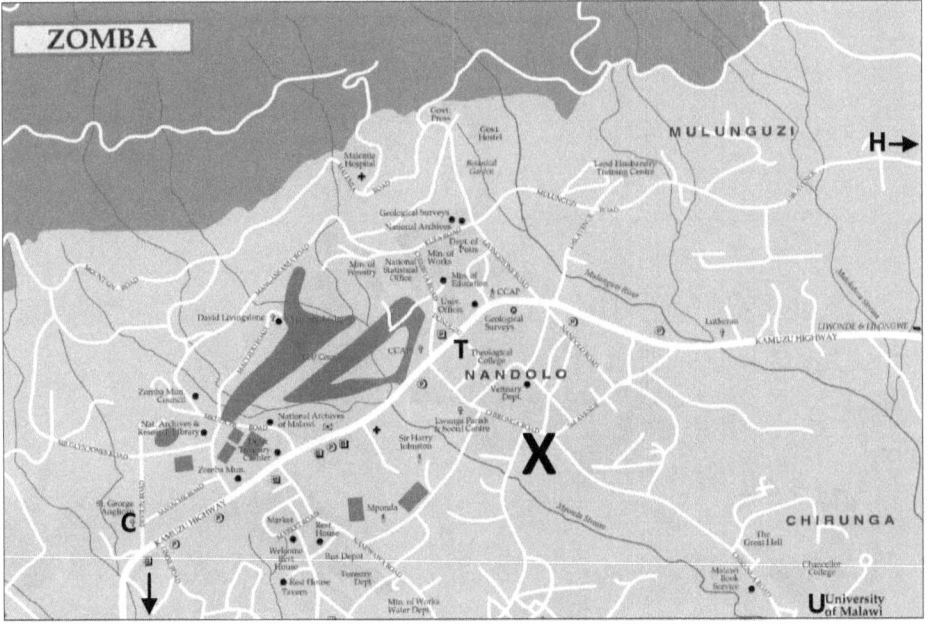

- **X** Anglican site for the projected Leonard Kamungu Theological College (LKTC)
- **C** St George's Anglican Church
- **H** Our house at the far end of Mulunguzi Road
- **T** Zomba Theological College (ZTC)
- **U** University of Malawi (UNIMA)
- **↓** *Zomba Catholic Cathedral and St Peter's Seminary are SW off the map.*

ZOMBA is a growing town in the Shire Highlands of Malawi, formerly the colonial capital. When President Kamuzu Banda moved government headquarters to its present more central location Lilongwe, a number of the redundant buildings were re-used for archives and various academic or research purposes. Some of them form part of the University of Malawi which Banda also founded. With secondary schools as well as Zomba Theological College and St Peter's Catholic Seminary, Zomba is thus the main educational centre in the country.

SINCE INDEPENDENCE in 1964, Malawi's population has grown 5 fold to around 13m – including many refugees from war-torn countries such as Mozambique. This has put great strain upon the infra-structure, land and lake resources, and the natural environment.

INTRODUCTION

Jacana
As seen in Liwonde National Park on an inlet from the Shire river.
Nearby were crocodiles!

Making a fishing net together

These villagers fish on the Shire river from dugout canoes.
In the background to the left is a *khola* (a house for doves)
and to the right of the *khola* is the goats' house.

PARTNERSHIP IN FAITH

IN THE 1850'S David Livingstone not only blazed a trail of exploration in Central Africa, but in a series of public addresses back in Britain set many hearts on fire for the missionary Gospel. His Cambridge speech of 1857 led to the founding of the Universities Mission to Central Africa (UMCA), whose aim was to combat the slave trade by encouraging alternative commerce and to implant church communities for the fostering of Christianity. After a further journey of 1859 in which he travelled via the Zambezi and its tributary the Shire River, Livingstone reached Lake 'Nyasa' (as he named it, a local word meaning 'lake'). He earmarked the Shire Highlands to the south of Lake Malawi (as it is now known) for a missionary settlement, and envisaged the introduction of cotton plantations trading their wares with Europe. Two years later Charles Mackenzie, an Anglican priest working in Natal, was consecrated by bishop Gray in Cape Town. As the missionary bishop of Central Africa he made his way with several colleagues to Magomero, a village halfway between present-day Blantyre, the commercial centre of Malawi named after Livingstone's birthplace in Scotland, and Zomba, a much smaller town housing the old parliament building, the university and the theological college, in colonial times the capital of the protectorate.

During his time at Magomero, Mackenzie enlarged his small mission by providing elementary schooling for a couple of dozen young Africans who had been freed from slavery. There was a particularly bright youth called Chimwala who was considered to have some potential for Christian leadership, although it was recognised that he would eventually need to travel south into Zululand for more formal training – assuming he was prepared to make the commitment.

There were numerous early setbacks, including Mackenzie's death within a year, and the difficulty of maintaining supply lines from the African coast. Livingstone, it appeared, had underestimated the hazards of river traffic, as well as the impact of disease and a restricted diet. The mission was withdrawn for a time, but a new impetus came with Livingstone's death in 1873. Indeed, a decade earlier John Keble, as he reflected on the abrupt ending of Mackenzie's heroic life, had even then foreseen the possibility of such fruition. 'Except a seed fall into the ground and die ...' were the words he inscribed in Mackenzie's much treasured and battered copy of *The Christian Year* after Charles' sister had retrieved it and shown it to the author.

The publicity surrounding Livingstone's demise encouraged UMCA to renew their mission in Central Africa in 1876, this time working inland from Zanzibar. There was a clear aim (in bishop George William Tozer's words) 'to train up some Africans to be missionaries to their own people'. A school of 'prophets' was begun in Zanzibar, with the intention of using such men as evangelists on the mainland. Eventually a secure base was established on Likoma Island between present day Mozambique and mainland Malawi. The most renowned of the missionaries was perhaps archdeacon William Percival Johnson, a fine Arabic scholar, who toiled on the eastern shores of Lake Malawi where he is still known as *Saint* Johnson. He travelled on foot and by boat, and began to see a distinct opening for a larger (multi-purpose) vessel. A mission ship, the *Chauncy Maples* was launched on the lake in 1901. It was named after Johnson's colleague who had become bishop in 1895 but who alas! drowned shortly afterwards in the waters of the lake, when his attempts to swim to safety after a shipwreck were frustrated by the cassock he was wearing. The new ship served as a hospital and sometimes as a place of temporary refuge from Arab slave traders; but for Johnson it was a school where promising recruits could be prepared for pastoral and missionary work – a theological college in embryo.

Other locations for training were used over the decades that followed the 1st World War. St Andrew's College was established on Likoma Island; some able candidates were sent to St John's College in Lusaka in the 1950s; while in the 1960s an ecumenical training centre was established at Chilema close to the new diocesan headquarters at Malosa, not many miles from Zomba. A number of existing catechists and teachers were given six months of preparation here before being ordained priest, and allowed to serve on half-pay. There was then a further development which was known in England as 'non-stipendiary ministry' but in Malawi as 'voluntary priesthood'. Ecumenical cooperation with the Catholic Church allowed a number of men to study at Kachabere Seminary near Mchinji during the 1970s, but as the number of Catholic seminarians grew there was less room for guest students from the Anglican Church. In time a handful of priests pursued higher degrees abroad. At one time UMCA had even contemplated bringing ordinands to England for their formation. Decades of schooling in the country had successfully raised the level of educational attainment in at least some of the laity, calling for a matching improvement in clergy standards.

Today the Anglican Church of Malawi (ACM) is flourishing and growing, although it remains financially constrained. Its three dioceses have upwards of twenty men in training for ordination at Zomba, where the Theological College (ZTC) is a joint venture with the Presbyterian Church (CCAP). Many others benefit from the rapidly expanding work of TEEM (Theological Education by Extension in Malawi), which began in 1979 and is run from the same Zomba campus. ACM maintains a 'catholic' witness to the faith, and when I go out (with my wife Sarah) in January to join the staff there my brief is particularly to support and strengthen this witness. The emphasis will be both doctrinal and pastoral.

Although the slave trade has long since disappeared, economic hardship remains, and now AIDS is ravaging the country. It is estimated that within the next decade perhaps half of the working population will be at serious risk, leaving thousands of orphaned children and depriving schools, farms, hospitals, businesses, and government administration of experienced staff. The Church clearly has a vital role to play. Good caring priests rooted in the Gospel and with imaginative powers of leadership are needed as never before. I hope our presence in Malawi will in a small way reaffirm the historic partnership between our two Churches, and that Catholic Anglicans in this country will care as much today as the pioneering fathers did a hundred and more years ago.

I shall be reporting next on a brief preliminary visit which is planned to take place in October 1999. Thereafter we hope to send back monthly reports, which – with a developing readership – may occasionally need to recap on 'the story so far'. So apologies to those who are with us from the very start!

FIRST IMPRESSIONS
November 1999

MALAWI IS FULL OF SURPRISES for the first-time visitor. There are many curiously worded signs adorning shops and other premises. I am told that a *The Hang-Over Pharmacy* is found in a number of villages, but perhaps not all can boast *The Tarmac View Resthouse*. In St. Thomas' Church, Lilongwe on the day after my arrival, it was astonishing to see a full church divided equally between men on the one side and women on the other, nearly all well under the age of 50 – because of course, sadly, few achieve any greater age. Apart from the priest just turned 60, I was the oldest person present. In the mass there was sparing use of candles, because of their cost, and likewise (throughout Malawi) communion is distributed by intinction to save expense on wine. The practice also reflects a widespread reverence for the Blessed Sacrament, and is not driven, as some suggest, by the fear of AIDS being transmitted.

While in the capital Lilongwe I was able to use the house of an American missionary away on leave. Having been troubled in Lesotho (some 15 years earlier) chiefly by rodents, I hadn't expected quite so many insects to be sharing my lodging. The shower in particular accommodated a huge colony of cockroaches – so when I went with bishop Peter to a Mothers Union rally in Nkhotakota down by the lake a few days after my arrival and stayed in a hospital guest room, I was well prepared to deal with similar forms of low life who joined me there! It was, however, a little alarming one morning in Lilongwe when the bishop called at the fish market on the way back to his house. We approached it via Devil Street, and then had to pass down a narrow alley: 'I'll go in front,' he advised, 'with you in the middle and our driver right behind you. That way you should be safe.'

My final few days were spent at bishop James' guesthouse in Malosa, headquarters of the diocese of Southern Malawi. In the bishop's absence, it was his wife who took me into Zomba to meet staff at the ecumenical theological college (ZTC), situated not far from the magnificent campus of Chancellor College – part of the University of Malawi. By now I had become aware of considerable unease about the existing partnership here with the Presbyterian Church. Before the college was set up over twenty years ago, Anglican seminarians had received their formation in various locations – at Catholic seminaries such as Kachabere or in neighbouring countries such as Zambia – and had hoped to develop the links with the Roman Catholic Church. But (as I had learnt in Lesotho) it was the presence of ordinands' wives that caused the Catholic authorities to have misgivings. The Catholic seminary of St Peter on the other side of Zomba, a mile or more out of town, remains a separate establishment, although there are regular contacts with it. In earlier, less ecumenical, days there was strong Presbyterian opposition to the arrival of Catholic missionaries, since Nyasaland (as it was then known) was regarded as Protestant territory. To avoid friction, the authorities insisted that Catholic missions should be at least twenty miles from every urban centre, a figure reduced in 1912 to a mere three miles – hence the present location of St Peter's seminary. UMCA, I am glad to note, was more sympathetic. There is an entry, dated 8 October 1890, in the Mponda Mission Diary of the White Fathers:

> The king has forbidden us to visit his people in their huts. We look after the sick who come to the mission. We are learning their language. The Anglicans have given us a grammar book which they wrote as well as a translation of the New Testament. They help us as much as they can and there is no hostility towards us.

I was heartened to learn that ecumenical cooperation has improved very considerably from those early beginnings, with church leaders consulting together regularly at a national level, and – at least in Zomba – the main churches joining forces each Good Friday in a united procession of witness all around the town. ZTC's location is perhaps symbolic, lying halfway between the nearest Catholic and Presbyterian churches.

The disquiet with the current theological affiliation in Zomba with Presbyterians has several aspects. First, the three Presbyterian Synods of Malawi have very different foundational histories, resulting in a degree of suspicion, even at times disharmony, amongst themselves. Perhaps the key unresolved issue is the degree to which their mutually inherited Calvinism can or must be adapted to meet changing circumstances. Of more immediate significance, their concept of formation is by no means the same as generally understood and practised by Anglicans. The Presbyterian emphasis is more narrowly academic, with too much attention seemingly devoted to bygone disputes within Western Europe and too little consideration given to prayer and spirituality. Preparation for wide-ranging pastoral care seems to have diminished compared with earlier decades, and there is apparently little concern about the expression of Christian faith in terms that resonate with African culture. Common worship is something of a problem, since Anglican use of traditional forms is disregarded and there is simply incomprehension of the needful centrality of the Eucharist.

However, a new opportunity will soon present itself for Anglican seminarians to live in their own community on a site owned by the Anglican Church further down the same road. In Zomba there is currently a massive project, now nearly completed, to enlarge the Mulunguzi Dam on the edge of the mountain plateau 1000 feet above the town, from which it draws its water supply. This is funded by the World Bank, with the contractor's complex of offices and warehouses occupying much of the site in question. When the project is complete, which is anticipated by the end of next year, all these recently constructed buildings will under the terms of the lease revert to the diocese of Southern Malawi. It is then intended to convert them into suitable student accommodation, along with classrooms, an office, a library and a chapel. Although it is expected that cooperation with Presbyterians would continue (for example, in the provision of lectures), a separate Anglican college would thus be able to establish a more coherent Anglican ethos.

It is on this new site that our house is to be built. £10,000 has already been donated for this purpose by the Community of the Resurrection, who have a significant presence in Southern Africa. Before visiting Zomba I had been informed by 'usually reliable sources' that its foundations had been dug and its walls had now reached window height. When I found nothing but a freshly ploughed field, I was somewhat nonplussed and not entirely convinced by the assurance that 'builders work very fast in Malawi'. It was not easy (such is the genial optimism so prevalent in Africa) to exact the admission that it would certainly not be ready in time for our arrival. In fact, I discovered that planning permission had not yet been obtained. Fortunately, when I dropped into a local cafe known as Caboodle, I met an Irish girl working for an NGO who came up with a suggestion: 'Why don't you contact a couple at the college who've just returned to Northern Ireland for six months' leave? You could probably use their house until yours is ready.' Acquiescence with this idea was indeed readily forthcoming when I made contact with the lecturer and his wife a week or so before getting back to England – so we shall after all have a temporary roof over our heads from January onwards.

Apart from developing the projected college buildings, a further challenge will be to equip them appropriately. I suspect some liturgical furnishings will be needed, and a new library will almost certainly have to be assembled. More of this anon, but meanwhile if there are retired priests with books to spare, or others who could help, I should be glad to hear. On the basis of my house hunting experience, it occurs to me that progress on the new college may be much slower than is presently anticipated, especially if there is a delay in making the necessary funding arrangements.

The Anglican Church cannot afford to train all the priests it needs. Every year, only a few of the men who offer can be accepted. An interesting experiment is underway in the Lake diocese, with two candidates for the priesthood being tutored by Father Rodney Hunter, whom I met briefly in his house at Matamangwe while heading towards Nkhotakota. Fr Rodney was my predecessor at ZTC and previously taught at Kachabere Catholic Seminary. (Over a cup of tea he explained much of the background being related here). Distance learning material from TEEM is being used in this provisional scheme, but whether it proves satisfactory with tutors other than Fr Rodney who has copious theological resources of his own is another matter. The hope is that an avenue will be found to enable men to be trained for the priesthood non-residentially and hence more affordably.

The need to explore alternatives that will complement the work at Zomba is obvious, when so many areas of the country are showing signs of growth. Father Howard of St. George's, Zomba told us on his brief visit to Birmingham that he now has 30 outstations over a wide area, and finds it increasingly difficult to keep in touch with all of them. Similar stories can be told elsewhere, especially in the deep south towards Mozambique where Anglican congregations are multiplying. In other places, too, there are tales of Muslims being converted – but seldom the reverse despite the allegiance of the President to the faith of Islam, who perhaps recognises the political repercussions for himself were he to be more actively partisan. I was very encouraged to see the number of church schools up and down the land, even though their premises and equipment are too often rudimentary, inadequate for the large class sizes. I was struck by the children's enthusiasm to learn: when they see *azungus* like myself, their request is more often for pencils and biros than for money.

Hardship is never far away, and even during my ten days in the country there was news making matters worse. First, unusual winds on Lake Malawi have disturbed the currents and brought apparently 'toxic' substances nearer the surface, rendering most fish somewhat unpalatable – the one exception being the delicious chambo. (NB. Archbishop Robert Runcie once visited Malawi and thanked his hosts for allowing him to taste their wonderful *chamba* – which is also found near the lake, being the illegally grown Indian hemp. Much laughter, I was told, ensued. At the present time, I gather some local farmers are turning to *chamba* as a more reliable cash crop than tobacco.) Since so much protein comes from the lake, and so many derive their living from fishing, this will be a hard blow. Then, just before I left, petrol and diesel prices were raised without warning by some 25%. This will undoubtedly push other prices upwards, and again make life more difficult. Thank God therefore that adequate rainfall is forecast for the growing season – and thank God for so much appreciation of his goodness in a land where fear, disease and deprivation are otherwise prone to take their toll.

Please pray for bishops Jack, Peter and James and all their people in upholding faith and hope, and for the priests of yesterday, today and tomorrow.

YEAR 2000

Purplecrested Lourie
As seen frequently in our garden,
where they love eating berries from one particular tree.
They are very colourful and make a repeated sound
like a cork being pulled out of a bottle.

A family kitchen
On the left, maize kernels are being separated from husks
(which are fed to animals although people eat them when food is scarce).
The maize is then cooked in a large pot balanced on three large stones.
It is eaten with *ndiwo*, a relish of tomatoes, beans, greens or meat.

DRINKING IN THE ATMOSPHERE
January 2000

AS NEWCOMERS we are still onlookers, drinking in the African atmosphere while coming to terms with the different climate and local difficulties such as water being cut off for most of the day. Our present accommodation is temporary, but is blessed with a garden full of trees and shrubs, including a mango tree and an avocado pear tree bearing a profusion of fruit.

Captivating birdsong and insect sounds are unfamiliar but fascinating. Monkeys swing from the branches, while lizards climb up the walls and noisy guinea fowl strut across our grass. Zomba plateau looms above us, often enveloped in mist, while the countryside around has become green and lush. When we arrived and concluded our journey with the internall flight from Lilongwe to Blantyre, the ground below looked very brown and parched. Since then it has rained most days, so the prospects for the maize harvest are looking much better. Not enough rain has yet fallen, however, to replenish the streams adequately for the coming dry season.

Cooking and hygiene are priorities and it is a challenge to make the best use of local produce, for example pawpaws, guavas, mangoes, tamarillos, cassava, pumpkin leaves, groundnuts and maize flour. Bargaining in Zomba market, which is open every day, certainly helps to improve our Chichewa. We've bought goat meat there – a novel experience – as well as a live free-range hen: the latter proved to be well-muscled and therefore extremely tough! One surprise is that liver is highly prized here as a food to nurture children, and is therefore much more expensive than (say) steak. The market, I should explain, offers far more than stalls selling meat and produce, and is a hive of many other activities such as welding and metal working. In the house, drinking water has to be boiled, flour checked for weevils, clothes ironed well to eradicate putsi fly eggs and, as always, mosquitoes kept at bay.

We have had a warm welcome both at college and at St George's Church. Hardly a day passes without people calling, looking for work, selling carvings or vegetables (yesterday, even a live hen strapped to a bicycle) or simply wanting money. One man comes regularly to collect empty bottles, tins and waste paper which he sells in the market to buy bibles for a village school. We see orphan children and cripples alike among the beggars outside the shops.

Women are everywhere carrying buckets of water or huge baskets of produce on their heads, possibly with a baby on their backs, and – as like as not – holding a large umbrella, either for shade from the sun or to keep off the rain. We understand, however, that skilful though they are at performing these feats, there is a risk of serious neck or back injury developing over time. By the roadside there are many wicker and grass stalls for produce or craft to be sold, sometimes along with useful items like soap or cheap utensils. One of the biggest contrasts to England is the daily spectacle of children as young as five streaming along the side of a busy road on their way to school. No car-rota or lifts for them! On Sundays many of the children are decked in their best clothes for church, which often means colourful bridesmaid dresses for the girls or page-boy suits for the boys – second-hand clothes, of course, that are now in such abundance in the marketplaces here, courtesy of aid organisations.

We gather that compared with (say) ten years ago, when our students at ZTC wore clothes until they were threadbare, these readily available and inexpensive imports have quite transformed their appearance, making frayed collars largely a thing of the past. The downside is that cotton growers have seen prices for their crops plummet, with the prospects for a viable local cotton manufacturing industry vanishing as rapidly as the imported clothes have arrived. One sensible initiative from the United States was to offer Third World countries the opportunity to sell manufactured goods there for five years free of the usual tariffs, but the Malawi government rejected the offer on the grounds that the only entrepreneurs likely to benefit would all be Asians.

This is a very different country from Lesotho, our previous African posting. There is so much to delight in but so many problems too and much more poverty than we saw in Southern Africa in the 1980s. There is still a serious battle to be won against witchcraft and superstition. Each week the local papers tell horrifying accounts of ritual killings, with the savage dismemberment of people's bodies. Witch-finders continue at considerable expense to be called in – even by church members – to point an accusing finger at someone supposedly causing injury or sickness to others. By no means all ministers of the gospel know where they stand on this issue and one is left wondering whether there is adequate determination by the churches to counter these malpractices, deeply rooted in the collective psyche. There is even a reluctance to talk openly about HIV/AIDS which is rampant in the country with devastating effects. Fear and ignorance make it so much harder for its spread to be contained.

Is the answer to come instead from better education, adequate health services and scientific enlightenment? If so, the wait may be long because Malawi has a significant social divide between the few affluent university graduates, at ease with the modern world and its technology, and the vast majority who live from hand to mouth, often going hungry and unable to afford even basic health care. Those who talk glibly of the IT revolution transforming our existence should remember that 97 per cent of the world has no access to it and aspire only to such simple requirements as a reliable supply of clean water.

We knew something about the situation here before we came. Experiencing it for ourselves is a different thing altogether. And there is much of which we were previously unaware: for example, that another killer disease has recently moved up from Mozambique, namely cerebral malaria, which is fatal if not treated within the first few hours. So Malawi is a world apart from England, where life is far from easy for the majority of people.

Please pray for open discussion and increasing awareness about AIDS – and of course for the vast majority in Malawi, living from hand to mouth.

AN OVERVIEW OF THEOLOGICAL TRAINING
February 2000

THE FIRST TRAINING for Anglican ordinands in Malawi happened over a hundred years ago. William Johnson's dream was to evangelise the villages bordering Lake Malawi, using a boat as his travelling home. It should be appreciated that this Lake, at 365 miles long and sometimes 40 or 50 miles wide, is the third largest in Africa, and that even today water transport is often preferable to the use of land tracks. Always on the move, Johnson realised that he also needed to educate future leaders of the church. So what better than to commission a larger boat, equipped with cabins for his students? There was a warm response in England to his appeal for funds and the new vessel was duly launched. Just one problem ... a hardy Oxford oarsman himself, Johnson had good sea legs but the African tribesmen found the turbulence of Lake Malawi more than they could stomach and often took to their bunks. Hence the experiment lasted only until the outbreak of the first World War, when the *Chauncy Maples* was commandeered for duty, and was not repeated once the war was over.

Zomba Theological College (ZTC), as it now is, came into being in 1977, on a convenient site in what had until recently been the capital of Malawi. Further down the same road is the University of Malawi with which ZTC has close links. On the college campus is an administration block with six lecture rooms and a separate wives' school. There is accommodation for both married and single students as well as for staff. A crèche is under construction. The latest addition is the library block, opened in 1994. Attached to it is a small hall intended to be used for study purposes but which serves at present as the college chapel. Since the government has recently returned land belonging to the college, it may at some point in the future be possible for a proper chapel to be erected here.

In the first year, ordinands have to leave their families behind and come to live together in a block known as 'the monastery.' Thereafter, wives and children move in to a number of two bedroom family units and the wives undertake a full programme of their own, including bible study, basic Christian teaching, pastoral work – and learning how to answer the telephone! For a few of them it is the first formal education they have ever received. An Irish missionary who has been in Malawi for 30 years runs this women's programme.

There are about 90 ordinands here, slightly more than in any English theological college. The Anglican Church in Malawi sends two or three each year from each of the three dioceses, roughly 24 in all. A few come from the Churches of Christ, one or two from Zambia and Zimbabwe and we have one Methodist from Mozambique. The majority of students are Malawian Presbyterians. Each of the three Presbyterian synods has its own background and traditions. Cooperation between them can, at times, be rather strained because of this. In the south, Blantyre Synod maintains strong links with the Church of Scotland whereas, in the north, Livingstonia Synod (associated with the famous Dr Laws) was founded by the Free Church of Scotland. In the middle is the ultra conservative Nkhoma Synod, an offshoot of the Dutch Reformed Church in South Africa.

ZTC is affiliated to the University of Malawi, which has its own religious studies department. Affiliated under the same diploma and degree programmes are several other training institutions, such as the Baptist Theological College and St Peter's Roman Catholic Seminary, on the far side of Zomba, but also establishments such as St John's Catholic Seminary elsewhere in the country. The university validates the diploma, which is the basic course undertaken by all students, and (as from 2001) the BD which will be available for those who are more academically able. The Malawi School Certificate (roughly equivalent in standard to the former O level programme in the UK) is the basic academic entry requirement, with at least four credits.

The diploma itself requires 15 credits over the three year period in college. BD candidates will be required to transfer after their second year and have a fourth year of study. There are a number of core subjects – such as biblical studies, church history and doctrine – and then a variety of options, such as Hebrew or Greek. TEEM (Theological Education by Extension in Malawi) provides the same programme through distance learning for qualified candidates, who need not necessarily be ordinands.

As well as the academic work, ordinands undertake a six week parish placement each year which is carefully reviewed throughout the period of residence. Leading worship and musical skills are emphasised in regular weekly sessions and one of my special responsibilities is to look after the Anglican students and induct them further into Anglican practices. We meet separately for a weekly mass and on most days say the evening office together. A period is set aside each Friday for Anglican studies, in which a range of topics is covered, such as the sacraments, Anglican history, traditions and spirituality. Shortly, we shall be going on a weekend retreat in Limbe and later we will visit Mua, the celebrated Catholic inculturation centre which houses a renowned museum of traditional customs and crafts.

There are seven full time staff. It is the bishops' hope that two of us will be Anglicans. This obtains briefly in this first term of 2000 but Fr Henry Mbaya will shortly return to South Africa to continue his doctoral studies and it will be some time before a Malawian priest is able to take his place. Where possible, the clergy are encouraged to study for higher degrees, usually in Britain or the USA. Bishop James Tengatenga himself has a master's degree from Texas and is completing a doctoral dissertation. In Zomba, because of the turnover of staff (at least three of the seven will have left by the end of the year) it is helpful to be academically versatile. At present, my main responsibilities are to teach New Testament to Year 1, church history to Year 2 and Christian ethics to Year 3.

Although there is, rightly, a concern to maintain good academic standards, the Anglican bishops sense that not enough emphasis is placed upon priestly formation. I take time in almost every class to reflect upon the implications for the life and mission of the church today but this is seen as a novel approach. Too many of the students set their sights no higher than absorbing quantities of information which they aim to reproduce in examinations. They are sometimes shocked when told that some of the details are unimportant, so long as they have grasped the main thrust of the argument or have understood the key principles. This was equally true in the 1980s in the seminary in Lesotho, and reflects a different educational system.

I hope we can move towards a more integrated programme in which theological studies connect better with the life that clergy will lead in their future ministry. But I suspect progress will be slow. In England, theological colleges are inspected every five years and regularly review their programmes and priorities. It is not clear to me that anything similar happens here – or is likely to happen. There is a college board of church leaders, but their time is usually devoted to finance, staffing and buildings. Within the college there is no real mechanism for discussing new approaches or ideas.

Shortage of money does not help the situation. Things we take for granted in England are often hard to come by here. At present the office fax machine and computer are both out of commission. There are no funds available to pay for their repair. I predict that the photocopier will break down soon through lack of maintenance. Students are, I am pleased to report, given a basic text book in each of the subject areas but it is evident that not many new additions are made to the library. The collection of older works is, however, fairly substantial – rather more extensive than what is available in the nearby library at Chancellor College.

For the most part, I find the students very responsive and keen to pursue their studies. Colleagues are extremely hospitable and friendly. From further afield come reports almost every day of new church ventures getting underway. There are many development projects and many dedicated Christian people who are bringing about real changes. For example, it is estimated that the churches maintain 80 per cent of the country's health programmes. At ZTC I hope we are preparing ordinands to be real spiritual and pastoral community leaders, able to inspire faith, hope and love in their people, sufficient to face the many challenges and to seize the opportunities for Christian outreach and mission that arise.

Please pray for the staff and ordinands at Zomba Theological College – and for openings to discuss new approaches and ideas.

THE COMMON GOOD
March 2000

DR HASTINGS KAMUZU BANDA came to power in Malawi in 1964, and ruled it with a rod of iron for the next 30 years, eventually being known as the Life-President. As one who had studied in South Africa, USA and UK (where he practised for quite a long time as a GP), he admired the Western way of doing things, and in one sense perpetuated, rather than replaced, the ethos of colonialism. Plato in his *Republic* had advocated rule by an elite band of philosophers, and Dr Banda set about the governance of Malawi in this way. He founded Kamuzu Academy to be the Eton of Africa, where the brightest young men and women should receive an education equal to the best offered in any English school. It was staffed almost exclusively by expatriates, and there was a rule that any African staff should vacate the premises during the hours of darkness, lest they pollute their charges with subversive ideas. Our tutor in New Testament Greek here in the Theological College was one of Banda's prize pupils. She attributes her success to the compulsory bowl of Corn Flakes each morning for breakfast! She recalls too the Latin used on Speech Day and how Dr Banda once upset the university staff in Zomba by complaining of the lack of classics there – essential in his eyes for any university worthy of the name. He was certainly prone to introduce Latin tags into his own speeches.

The Kamuzu Academy elite became in time Banda's senior colleagues and officials, appointed to run the country efficiently. Their salaries were large, but in turn they were expected to be incorruptible and to deliver a safe and adequate environment for the rest of the population. Indeed, there was little crime, and poverty was not as extreme as in many other African countries. The downside was the silencing of any opposition and the suppression of independent thinking. Dr Banda was ruthless with those whom he felt to be a threat. Among religious groups it was the Jehovah's Witnesses who were singled out especially, and reports of them being fed to crocodiles in the Shire river are credible. In every town and village, no matter how small, the Youth League reported on most activities and eavesdropped even on private conversations. Banda's Pioneers applied any necessary corrective intimidation or violence, although foreigners regarded as unsympathetic to the regime were simply expelled. There is a story of an American discussing politics back in his home country at a dinner party who then remarked that in his view it was time for the President to resign. The cook who overheard this comment misinterpreted it as criticism of Dr Banda and duly reported him. Within a day or two the American had been forced to leave the country!

For most of his reign, Dr Banda was regarded as a reliable ally by Western governments, and received substantial amounts of aid. With the issue of human rights starting to take centre stage in the world, however, relations with (for example) the UK cooled. When the Roman Catholic bishops in Malawi issued their highly critical pastoral letter and were arrested for their pains, the volley of external criticism coupled with the suspension of aid finally brought about Banda's demise, followed by the first democratic elections in 1994. Aid then started to flow again, and Malawi now receives in direct aid alone about USD550 million each year (or USD50 per head of population). Western countries are committed to proving that democracy works better than dictatorship.

If only it were so simple! As in former communist countries in Eastern Europe (or in Russia herself) there is all the chaos and instability of transition. In six years, corruption, crime and violence have become commonplace. In that time the natural environment, once carefully protected, has become visibly degraded. Whole hillsides have been stripped bare of trees. Bilharzia has become a serious risk in Lake Malawi because of overfishing there, and it is even more common around Lake Chilwa, where villagers now assume that blood in one's urine is normal. In places of education teachers are noted for absenteeism, with examination results plummeting.

The government, depending as it does on a popular mandate to stay in power, is unwilling to get tough. It should know well enough what measures are needed, given the number of funded ministerial seminars that have taken place, but it lacks the courage to challenge the now universally held notion that 'multi-party democracy means everyone can do what he likes'. As for the funds that continue to pour into the country, it is clear that the theory of the 'trickle-down' effect is no more applicable in

Africa than in any other continent. Whereas under Banda the elite numbered perhaps 5% of the population, now as many as 20% can be reckoned wealthy – but the gap between them and the poor has widened. In fact, the differential between rich and poor is greater in Malawi than in almost any other country of the world. If the average wealth of the richest 20% is compared to that of the poorest 20%, in most Western countries the ratio is typically around 6:1; in Malawi it has been estimated as 38:1.

Campaigns for a fairer world, such as Jubilee 2000 (a cause well worth supporting), do not always make adequate allowance for the scale of corruption in 3rd World countries – for example, the danger of overseas assistance ending up in the wrong pockets or being applied to inopportune prestige projects. This year the government auditor revealed that at least one-third of public funds – and therefore probably as much as one-half – is misappropriated in Malawi. If this figure sounds scandalously high, consider the situation elsewhere in Africa: (1) wealthy Nigerians have more than enough money in Swiss bank accounts to pay off that country's entire foreign debt, while (2) in Kenya funds that have left the country over the past 25 years for private investment more than outweigh the inflow of overseas aid during that same period. But easy though it is to point accusing fingers at crooked African ministers, civil servants and businessmen, the truth is that there are also plenty of scandals waiting to be unearthed back in the UK. I recall conversations with regular churchgoers in our last parish who were only too ready to dismiss the African continent as a lost cause while refusing to apply the same ethical standards to their own government and business leaders.

In my ethics class we drew up a list of the most urgent moral issues facing Malawi, and each week now the students present their findings and conclusions on each one in turn. It is evident that the fear instilled by the Banda regime will take some time longer to be eradicated. Caution, more than anything else, prevails. Few students are prepared now or seemingly in the future to challenge the rampant abuses they see. 'Our own family, our own church leaders, are also implicated,' they say, 'so we look on but dare not speak.'

It is obvious that the media too is very much constrained. If ministerial misconduct is ever reported, it rapidly disappears from public view, never to be mentioned again – unlike the situation in the UK, where journalists leave no stone unturned to get to the bottom of things. To attempt something similar in Malawi would be to expose oneself to a violent attack upon one's house, one's car or one's person – at the hands of unknown government supporters. Apart from the few newspapers there is also a radio service controlled by the state together with a television network in its infancy: the latter is largely a vehicle for displaying the activities of the President and his family (and is very boring to watch).

Many questions are therefore left unanswered. How can one compare the repressive, but moderately effective, regime with its liberal, but incompetent, successor? Does democracy really bring the peace, the justice, the freedom, that is much to be desired? How far should external pressures be brought to bear upon the internal policies of a country – and if they are, can they really achieve much significant change? One thing that Christians ought to know is the deviousness of the human heart and the complexity of human actions. There are no simple – and certainly no simplistic – solutions to our political or to our personal problems. Whatever grand designs may be proposed, there will be a hundred and one ways in which they fail to address the practical realities, or in which they may be undermined by vested interests.

Yet as Christians that is no reason to give up our faith in God's own purposes. The dilemmas we face here, as in most African countries torn apart by the rapid change of circumstance, at root reflect the ambiguities of the human condition. While we appear to be free, we are not truly able to fashion the future even as we would desire it for ourselves. And even when we think to have improved life for the majority, there will be some who suffer injury in the process or who slip through the net, while others will exploit the benefits to their own advantage. So how do we attain what the Catholic Church knows as 'the common good'? Is it best left to individuals to be motivated through and through with a love of their fellow human beings, or must a corporate version of that love be more forcefully expressed in the public arena? Further thoughts on this to follow ...

Please pray for a common sense of purpose within Malawi, in which resources and opportunities are fairly shared.

BREAKING THE SILENCE
April 2000

IN A RECENT BOOK on Christianity in Africa Paul Clifford explored the relationship between churches and the state in a number of different countries. He concluded that it was those churches which had international connections which were able to stand relatively clear of governmental interference and to exercise more moral leverage than many of the locally initiated churches.

Although Malawi was not one of the countries featured in his research, nowhere was this truer than here in the early 1990s. Dr. H. K. Banda was by then a very old man, having exercised an increasingly ruthless life-presidency for three decades. The accounts of his later megalomania are astonishing. When he visited a town or village, life there had to stop for the day – shops and schools had to close. When he drove along the highway, he would be preceded by a police cavalcade making sure that all other traffic halted and pulled off the road. The occupants had to get out and stand respectfully by the roadside singing patriotic songs. On Martyrs' Day (3rd March) smiling was a punishable offence, and as there were many paid informers it was prudent to keep a straight face. A senior figure in the national Geological Survey told me recently of an even more bizarre manifestation of Banda's hubris. Having once announced that Malawi had few mineral resources, he was not prepared to modify this statement in the light of further geological exploration. So, when significant finds of 'rare earth' deposits were discovered in the hills north of Blantyre, those in the know had to keep this information to themselves for fear of exposing the President's fallibility.

Of course, all this was but the outward appearance of a regime long past its sell-by date. There was gross injustice in the way public funds were spent, if not siphoned off for grandiose presidential projects. Yet overseas aid kept pouring in, as Banda was regarded as a reliable pro-western ally. Within the country there was widespread disillusionment, but with Banda's spies everywhere no one dared to voice criticism.

As noted last month, it was the Catholic Bishops who eventually broke the silence in 1992 and had a pastoral letter read out in all their churches, asking for justice and democracy – following which the floodgates of opposition were fully open. Soon British policy changed and aid was frozen, and with determined opposition on a wide front the MCP government was forced to allow multiparty elections in 1994. Unsurprisingly, they lost to the UDF headed by a Muslim businessman Bakili Muluzi who remains in office after winning a second (and disputed) round of elections last year.

Not all the change has been for the better. For example, while primary schooling is now free and a second university has been opened in Mzuzu, law and order are less in evidence. 'Multi-party democracy' has been interpreted by many as the end of all constraint, and, with weapons available at ridiculously low prices in the aftermath of the Mozambique civil war, armed robberies and violence have been sharply on the increase. There is some evidence that this is being brought, albeit slowly, under control – yet it's sad to see how wealthier Malawians, especially in the capital Lilongwe, try to insulate themselves from the problems by building high brick walls around their houses. It's also sad to observe the fleet of luxury cars that drive at terrifying speeds in the Presidential convoy, signalling the gulf that separates the ruling elite from ordinary Malawians.

Of greatest concern is the widely-held perception that the corrupt features of Banda's regime are being repeated under Muluzi. There are many stories of people being 'bought' by a personal gift from Muluzi himself. Those who have turned up to shake his hand may find themselves going away with an envelope stuffed with kwacha notes. Church leaders and their wives have also been compromised. Some have been given vehicles, others cash or mobile phones. While one Anglican bishop known to me refused the offer of a new car, there are reputed to be several Anglican priests who are better off for taking the President's side.

Given the low stipend – the equivalent of £40 per month – on which they struggle to feed their (often quite large) families, it is easy to appreciate their reasons for doing so. But when their phones are used to keep the UDF well informed about the political activities in their parishes, or even about the supposed political opinions of their bishop, it would seem that the price of collusion is too high.

In an atmosphere of mutual suspicion, it is now well-nigh impossible for church leaders to confer together about the situation in the country. It is understandable that Bishop Jack Biggers, an American who is retiring from the diocese of Northern Malawi in September, has suggested that it might be appropriate to appoint another expatriate, someone who can voice clearly and openly the concerns of his people. Indeed, it is the north that feels most neglected by the government, whose power-base is in the much more populous south. Here at college tensions are sometimes felt between students from different churches, but equally significant are the regional feelings, with northerners again under some pressure.

Paul Clifford's analysis suggests that it may have to be yet again the Catholic Church that comes to the rescue. Their particular strength is the presence in neighbouring Zambia of a Papal Nuncio, who can call the Catholic bishops together to confer. In theory the provincial structure of the Anglican Church should be able to facilitate a similar response, but in both Zambia and Zimbabwe the bishops face personal and political pressures of their own, which are unlikely to allow sufficient attention to be given to Malawi's difficulties. One would hope that religious leaders within Malawi could speak with a collective prophetic voice, but the weight of day-to-day administration and the considerable distances between them (which are not merely geographical) seem to make this an unlikely scenario. The real question though is, How many of them are already compromised?

Please pray for Christian leaders in all the churches of Malawi, that they may have the courage to speak up for their people and to live out gospel teachings.

JUBILEE SOUTH
May 2000

THROUGHOUT THIS YEAR, the issue of land redistribution in Zimbabwe has featured prominently in the news. What may not be so evident to European onlookers, though, is the wide measure of support that Robert Mugabe commands across Southern Africa i.e. support, if not for his chosen tactics, certainly for his broad strategy. This is closely linked to the different ways in which Jubilee 2000 is viewed from the North and from the South. It was launched in the countries of the North to relieve the poverty of those in the South, calling at first for debt relief. Soon, this became the stronger call for debt cancellation, despite the misgivings of campaigners who feared that if old debts could be disregarded so might new ones – to the discouragement of new lenders.

For nearly three years now, countries of the South have been much more active in the campaign, not least here in Malawi where the effects of capital outflows are seen on a daily basis. Where earlier debt cancellation was linked to structural adjustment programmes, now it is realised that this curtails government spending where it is needed most, on health and education. So Jubilee South goes deeper into the inequities of the world economy, exposing some of the flaws in the concept of 'free trade' as promoted by the World Trade Organisation. The demand for debt cancellation has been intensified by the additional call for *reparation* (or as the courts might put it, for 'damages') in compensation for the injuries inflicted on Third World societies over previous decades, and indeed longer. This is the context in which President Mugabe views white-owned farms in his country as truly belonging to the people of Zimbabwe, and insists that the former colonial power Britain should be the one to pay any financial compensation if they are taken over. In South Africa white-owned farms are just as much a target: although the pressure there is less extreme, many more white farmers have been killed than in Zimbabwe.

We detect similar stirrings here in Malawi. The government is considering legislation that would abolish any freehold of property, leaving those who own farms and estates with the insecurity of leasehold. Without very careful drafting such a law would upset many Malawians too, who have a strong attachment to their territorial rights. At times this can result in a lack of concern for any wider environmental responsibilities, particularly where tree cutting results in problems of flooding or the serious loss of habitats. Or again, those who earn a living by Lake Malawi tend to regard their fishing grounds as 'inalienable property', regardless of the impact upon fish stocks. Yet neither can the government act arbitrarily and may in the future need to be restrained when oil exploitation in the Rift Valley is further considered. Proposals to mine bauxite in the area around mount Mulanje have also raised serious concerns for those living there, although it now seems that the whole idea is economically unrealistic and unlikely to be implemented.

Given that white farmland handed over in the past has tended to end up in the hands of Mugabe himself or those of his cronies, a little cynicism about his motives – and correspondingly those of Malawi's ruling regime – is not unjustified. Do the poor of the land necessarily benefit from land reforms and developments? In Zimbabwe, for example, a 'white' farm may typically employ workers from around 200 families; their pay may well be meagre, but generally they will have job security together with some social benefits such as education for their children. Displace the farmer and give his land to 40 or 50 other families – who will then look after his former employees or give them jobs? How long will it take before the new landowners achieve the same output? Meanwhile, who will generate the country's wealth – and who will bear the hardships? There will surely be some success stories consequent upon land re-distribution, but the suspicion is that too many will lack the capital resources to make the most of their opportunities. At best, recovery will be long and slow, with a number of casualties *en route.*

Undeniably, throughout Southern Africa, and even in Malawi, there is a mood of anger against Europeans – a sense that these latecomers to the African continent stole the birthright of black people. Despite the fact that the colonial powers withdrew some 30 or 40 years ago, it is felt that their presence inflicted long-term damage upon African society and has continued to do the same through economic imperialism and now globalisation. If there is a new emphasis upon human rights and poverty relief, the race to grab agricultural and mineral resources is still on. Too often overseas investment serves only the strategic interests of the West, which also takes the lion share of the profits. Any that remain cannot in any case be guaranteed to benefit more than the corrupt few.

Theologically this same resentment is spelt out differently. There is much talk about Christ 'being in Africa' before Christianity came. There is a revival of interest in tribal customs, and the suggestion that family and community life would be much restored if the old ways condemned by the missionaries flourished once again. Students here at ZTC are turning against the churches' insistence upon monogamy. A Western code of ethics is not our style, they argue. Today the new missionary societies – the non-governmental organisations (of which at least one is likely to be found operating in most Malawian villages) – are felt to be imposing foreign ways and unacceptable values, despite the good that they do and the benefits that they bring. Some NGOs, for example, offer both their expatriate and their locally recruited staff a standard of living far beyond the wildest dreams of those they are helping.

Perhaps the key to facing the challenge before our students in college is to be found in Jesus' words, 'I came not to destroy but to fulfil.' The Christian faith should never be seen as a matter of spiritual imperialism. UMCA's own tradition was similar to that of the early Catholic missionary congregations (such as the Missionaries of Africa or the Montfort Fathers) in insisting on its priests living in simple African style and promoting an African Christianity. It struck me a few months ago when visiting the graveyard of All Saints, Nkhotakota that no one could ever accuse the young Anglican missionaries buried there of exploitation. Their grave stones record a number of deaths after perhaps only two or three years of service in Malawi, underlining their sacrificial commitment to the spreading of the gospel. They offered a *jubilee*, but its main focus was upon spiritual freedom, from fears of vengeful spirits, from sorcery and witchcraft, from family or tribal feuding. Alas! such oppressive fears have not yet been dispelled ...

Please pray that our students may enter more fully into 'the mind of Christ' as they engage with the pastoral challenges lying before them.

FAITH IN THE FUTURE
June 2000

WHATEVER THE PUBLIC HYSTERIA in Britain, hybrid food is certainly good news for Malawi. Two years ago about 25% of smallholders here were using hybrid maize seed; today the figure has risen to 75%, not because of pressure from the government nor through the blandishments of advertising, but because farmers are impressed with the results. Where previously (let us say) fifteen bags of corn were harvested, hybrid seed can double this figure. True, it takes much fertiliser if it is to flourish, so that a farmer has to sacrifice the equivalent of two bags to buy the necessary chemicals. But he can still produce vastly more than before. In other African countries smallholders can usually raise a separate cash crop to pay for such overheads: in Malawi, land is all too scarce. Other hybrid (or even genetically modified) developments may well help to improve the intake of essential vitamins and minerals: thus, in China, scientific advances now allow two billion people to benefit from rice that has been boosted to carry vitamin A, previously deficient in their diet.

There is another popular misconception that needs demolishing. It may be true in a few African countries such as Nigeria, and perhaps the Ivory Coast and Kenya, that outside donor assistance is nullified by the net outflow of funds. But even allowing for this deficit, Africa as a whole, and Malawi in particular, is genuinely better off because of aid loans and donations – which is not to deny that some of this money goes astray. (I recall here that in Zomba only last week pharmacists at the hospital were arrested for selling donated medicines on the black market.) Malawi and other Third World countries need all the targeted and well-monitored help that Western countries can give. There may be a small (and probably growing) minority of wealthier people but there are many more struggling to survive.

Very few Malawians are in paid employment, and most families exist on what they can grow themselves, cooked with fuel which they've collected from nearby. But the elderly and the handicapped, numbering about a quarter of the population, simply do not have the resources or the physical strength to work for a living, to grow their own food, or to take part in projects which reward the participants with 'food for labour'. They are certainly below the poverty line, and roughly as many again are in that category with them. Hence, until Malawi can support social welfare schemes, outside funds will be needed for the most vulnerable. However, identifying them fairly is easier said than done, and sometimes the local chief may enrich himself in their place. This is not an argument against offering financial assistance, but rather an indication that more reliable agencies (such as local churches) should be used in its distribution. It remains vital for outside help to be received on strictly accountable terms.

Relief assistance is also likely to be needed for the foreseeable future because of increasingly unpredictable weather patterns. Global warming seems to bring with it, not so much a recognisable change in local climates, as the growing prevalence of extreme conditions. Malawi was fortunate in being little affected by the recent floods in Mozambique, and was in fact, along with South Africa (which did itself suffer), first in the field with rescue helicopters. Curiously, though, while Mozambique was experiencing the most rain received in 50 years, Malawi in the last wet season has had the least rainfall in that same period. This contrast can remind us that weather patterns do change over the centuries, and it is worth remembering that Lake Malawi was much smaller in extent two or three hundred years ago, when the country must have experienced generally drier conditions. It is likely that in those days sorghum was the preferred crop, rather than maize which needs more rainfall. Actually, a very interesting phenomenon has occurred in the past 9 months on the Lake. Last August and September an unusual wind managed to alter the prevailing currents, bringing quantities of decomposed matter much nearer the surface. Starved of oxygen many fish died, and for several months the livelihood of fishermen was in jeopardy. Now, however, their fortunes have revived, because this richer food source in the lake has significantly increased the fish stock beyond the level that previously obtained.

Not everything, therefore, is bad news from Africa. Human beings, given training and motivation, can work together to overcome the setbacks and difficulties, and indeed nature has her own restorative powers. But farsightedness is needed, a wisdom that goes beyond political opportunism and even beyond technological capability. One illustration taken from Somalia half a century ago may make the point. Drought conditions are nothing new in Africa. In Somalia the people expected them to occur every so often, and made necessary preparations in advance. The chiefs would meet together, and would debate their contingency plans for days at a time. Eventually agreement would be reached as to which tracts of land should be set aside for emergency use. Anyone taking his animals to feed there without permission would then be shot! Hence, when disaster did befall, there was an untouched area available to sustain the herds through the time of crisis. It was an African solution to an African problem, and it depended very much upon an ordered social and political structure. One thing needed today throughout the continent is an adequate pool of such incorrupt and farsighted leaders.

The Church here has the task of fostering what Jonathan Sacks used as the title of his seminal book *Faith in the Future*. I take great encouragement from a pilgrimage made recently with a fellow Malawian priest. We followed country tracks for several miles away from the highroad, and then found local guides, as we went in search for Magomero, the short-lived site of the first mission to Central Africa back in 1861. A bottle was buried here that year containing a paper on which was written

> The first and corner post of the Church of St Paul was erected by Bishop Mackenzie and the Revs H. C. Scudamore and H. Rowley on this first day in October, in the year of our Lord one thousand eight hundred and sixty one, being the first anniversary of the departure of the Mission from England.

Dr Mellor's sketch of Magomero in October 1861

When I was directed to drive through a narrow strip of long grass between two maize fields I nearly lost heart. But there as we emerged into a clearing bounded by a loop of the Namadzi river, contrary to our expectations, was a living Anglican community. We knew that, before the end of his first year in Magomero, bishop Charles Mackenzie had gone down south to locate fresh medical and other supplies, but in vain. He died of fever on 31st January 1862, and when his companion returned to base after burying his body (one hundred years later to be reinterred in St. Paul's Cathedral, Blantyre) Fr Burrup also died of the same fever. There is a stone cross at Magomero marking his grave. That seemed to be the end and soon afterwards the mission was withdrawn.

In the following decade, however, renewed fervour led Anglican missionaries into Malawi from the east instead of the south. They made Likoma Island their headquarters. What we hadn't realised was that eventually a priest had visited Magomero again to renew the work there. A small new church was erected a stone's throw from Burrup's grave, and a congregation was quickly re-established. They were in good heart on the day of our visit. A choir of young people was rehearsing for the following Sunday, singing so exquisitely any cathedral in the world would have been honoured to hear them. I asked them about the dedication of the church. The answer came back unhesitatingly 'St Mackenzie's'. It was I'm sure the memory of his heroic determination that inspired them; and that even if his counter-offensive against the slave trade was ineffective in so far as he unwittingly handed control of this trade to the tribe who supported him, they knew that his heart was in the right place!

That story of restoration can, I believe, happen wherever the Church finds itself. Despite setbacks, despite inauspicious beginnings, God can be trusted to fulfil his mission. Our Christian faith assures us that despite our many blunders, God has the willingness and the love to recreate his world.

Please pray for the people of Magomero, and for Christians in Malawi expanding the horizons of God's church.

A CLASH OF CULTURES
July 2000

EACH WEEK THAT PASSES, we learn a little more about the country that is home to us for the time being. Wednesday afternoon is a particularly valuable opportunity when I listen to some of the practical experience gained by ordinands on placement. Nyau dancing featured this week, and is apparently still widespread in the central region. It is seen as a threat by all the Christian churches and by the Muslim community (10% of the population) alike.

If I have understood correctly, this type of dancing is a traditional feature of initiation ceremonies marking the transition from childhood to adulthood at the time of puberty. The dancers assemble under the authority of the local chief in the village burial ground. There they assume disguises, for fear of being recognised, but also because they represent not themselves but the spirits of the ancestors. Hence their faces are covered by masks, often with animal features. When they emerge, it is also with words and gestures that may be pointedly obscene, even by the standards of liberal western society. In theory, the 'good' characters represented are being held up for imitation, while 'bad' behaviour is exhibited to show the contrast. Nevertheless, Christian opinion seems to be that the results can only be expected to fall well short of Christian standards of morality, especially as the masked men go well beyond what may once have been permitted i.e. they terrorise the neighbourhood and are liable to attack and harass women during the allocated ceremonial days. There is also much condemnation of the sexual initiation of girls at puberty, who in some villages are still expected to copulate with a man known as *fisi* ('hyena'), which – at the very least – is a recipe for spreading HIV infection at an early age.

To judge thus is not of course to condemn initiation ceremonies out of hand. In some African countries traditional rites have been combined successfully with Christian training. In Malawi, however, it is generally otherwise, although an outstanding exception has evolved in Mangochi, just south of the Lake. Here male circumcision is carried out at puberty in the local hospital in conjunction with appropriate instruction from Catholic catechists. Yet, in a village where more colourful Nyau rituals take place, Christians will usually – if with difficulty – attempt to distance themselves. The risk they run is that, if the chief discovers youngsters who have not undergone the traditional initiation, they may well be attacked and driven from the village. There is a clear clash of cultures, in which the chief as guardian of local custom feels seriously threatened by the Christian stance.

It is hard to appreciate this very different rural scene from a seat of learning like Zomba, where the theological college and the university are both prominent institutions. There is a significant divide between those few who have been able to pursue more advanced studies, and so to be relatively at ease in the world of rational ideas and scientific analysis, and those many who are struggling at subsistence levels, for whom the spirit world is all too real and who live in fear of threatened reprisals. It takes some degree of education to reflect critically upon, and considerable self-confidence actually to challenge, the status quo.

It is noticeable that this applies in other walks of life as well. In the Church, for example, there is generally much greater respect for ordained ministers and leaders than obtains in Britain. A bishop here finds himself less readily challenged than in England. Indeed, African Anglicans hold the archbishop of Canterbury in vastly greater respect than many people in his own province. An overseas visit, one presumes, must be a most welcome break for him. Malawian Anglicans regard him as their father-in-God, and so are deeply shocked to discover how little he is esteemed by bishops (or even primates) elsewhere who are determined to pursue their own agenda heedless of his advice. There is a sense of privilege here in having received the Gospel, together with a sense of duty to transmit it faithfully to the next generation. People do not want to tinker with what is tried and tested, nor does theological or liturgical innovation have much appeal. They see themselves as stewards of a precious inheritance, and are dumbfounded by those who treat it casually.

However, as is evident from the last Lambeth Conference (in 1998), African bishops have not gained their stripes in the struggle against dark forces for nothing. Having received the light and truth of the Gospel, they are not going to jettison it in favour of dubious innovations justified only by

Western standards of political correctness. This for them is no less a threat than Nyau dancing – and coincidentally seems to exalt sexual licence and to treat its detractors with a similar ruthlessness. We are grateful therefore to live on this 'backward' continent with orthodox bishops who now safeguard the faith of their missionary fathers.

Thank God too that here in Zomba my academic colleagues have little inclination to dally with the latest fashions or fancies. I brought with me to Malawi several workbooks from one of our regional ordination courses, naively thinking that they might be of use. I was somewhat disturbed on reading them to discover both how little ground they covered and also into what ideological mould the reader was being directed.

One example of biblical exegesis concerning the 'medium' or 'witch' of Endor struck me as singularly unhelpful for Malawian ordinands, for whom witchcraft is a disturbing feature of daily life:

> The Medium of Endor is a minister of religion, and a good one. She understands the need of the one who comes to her, she takes charge of the situation, she does what she can for him. In her technical capacity she efficiently performs the appropriate ceremony and gives Saul a satisfaction he must have even though it can do him no real good.

Somehow that fails to inform an adequate Christian response to the phenomenon of Nyau rituals, or more widely to African traditional religion. Indeed, in affirming the medium of Endor as a 'good' minister of religion it surrenders any Christian critical faculties in order not to offend those who have other beliefs and practices.

As Pope John Paul wrote:

> We must not tamper with God's word. We must strive to apply the Good News to the ever-changing conditions of the world but, courageously and at all costs, we must resist the temptation to alter its content or reinterpret it in order to make it fit the spirit of the present age.

Please pray for bishops and church leaders who uphold the apostolic faith, and for those who strive to discover God's word for a generation who face changing or challenging circumstances.

PROTECTIVE MAGIC
August 2000

WHEN A BABY is born in Malawi it is customary for special charms to be hung about his or her person, to ward off any evil or sorcery that might injure them. In adulthood many Malawians continue to carry such charms in their pockets. Surprisingly, this includes many clergy and a significant number of church members. When challenged, an excuse may be proffered about not wanting to offend the parent or grandparent who gave them; but in reality there is still a widespread fear of witchcraft which a century and more of Christianity has hardly begun to check. A current college questionnaire, designed to glean some feedback from our students, asks 'Are you under any obligation to engage in protective magic if you feel vulnerable to witchcraft and sorcery in African congregations?' Before concluding – as was once the way in European circles – that the curse of Ham still rests upon the African peoples, one should pause to reflect on the measures some Westerners still take to bring better fortune into their lives, whether through the acquisition of New Age prophylactic charms or (in religious circles) through a mistaken faith in holy medallions or relics.

Every week I hear tales of witchery from those who have been on placement. When I suggest that it is not the sorcery itself but the fear of the sorcerer that does the damage, I am laughed out of court. More tales, based on first-hand experience, are regaled to drive home the potency of witchcraft. 'There were three brothers in our village. One died, leaving a widow. The remaining brothers quarrelled over whose wife she should be. Eventually the elder one gave in, but then put a curse on the other, threatening to "eat his bones". Within hours, this one lost the use of his legs, and seemed to be turning into jelly. They sent for the elder brother, who demanded the sacrifice of a cow to the appropriate local deity. This done, the villagers gnawed the bones and then threw them at the jellified younger brother. Instantly he recovered.' Or again, I heard about the rivalry between two church members, each of whom wanted to be in charge of the choir. Some months later the unsuccessful candidate lay dying and was heard by his son as saying, "That man is killing me." The son now firmly believes that this was what happened; he has ceased going to church until such time as the death has been avenged. The third story is of a couple of domineering church members, a man and his wife each holding a significant lay office, but letting it be known that no one would ever dethrone them with impunity. As the wife on one occasion was found drunk and disorderly, she was removed from her post as leader of the women's guild. But her replacement died within a few months, and she was then reinstated. Subsequently the husband was found in the same drunken state, but this time no one could be found willing to supplant him, for fear of a like fate – an unexpected early death.

Death, like any other reversal of human fortune, may have a medical or 'scientific' explanation, but if Malawians ever discover what it is – which is often unlikely given the shortage of doctors, and the expense and trouble of finding one – they will still look for a human cause. It is clear to many of them, for example, that AIDS is a particular form of sorcery that has been inflicted on Africa by Europeans as a substitute for direct colonial rule. Not long ago this accusation was publicly stated by the Prime Minister of Namibia!

The question Africans ask in the face of sickness or suffering is, 'Who is doing this harm? Who is working this magic against us?' As suspicion in domestic situations inevitably falls on colleagues and acquaintances, attendance at a family funeral, or at a neighbour's, is essential. One's absence would most naturally be attributed to guilt. People attend, of course, out of respect and to express sympathy, but there is usually an element of self-interest. With escalating numbers of AIDS-related deaths the negative impact on the work place has recently led the President to decree that traditional practices of mourning can be mitigated, and attendance at funerals need not extend beyond family members.

This does not, however, mitigate the tendency to pin the death on a scapegoat. A witch-finder may still be called in to detect the guilty party. Last year one Anglican congregation in the central region paid 8000 kwacha for such services (a sum equal to their annual quota payment to the diocese, which is considered burdensome and quite unattainable!). In fact anyone with a grasp of human nature and a nose for group dynamics could perform the role of a witch-finder with distinction. All that is necessary is to identify the person most disliked by other villagers, and to heap the blame on him or her (a conclusion reached also by Keith Thomas in his study of the witchcraft fears that came in the aftermath of the Reformation). The accusation should then be cloaked with suitably impressive theatricals. Props such as a live hen and a fusty pile of ash and bones are probably a *sine qua non*, so may well need to be planted by an accomplice.

Temporarily, this solves the problem. But few people are so isolated in society as to be without any family or friends at all, and it is seldom that only one person feels victimised. Seething resentment at the injustice makes for a lasting feud and fuels the desire for retaliation. Sooner or later the opportunity will occur for counter-accusations and some form of revenge. Hence one can note that, whether or not the exercise of witchcraft engages dark or magical forces, it is certainly a manifestation of human jealousy. Thus, the reason why, despite the advent of Christianity and of a degree of literacy and education, sorcery persists here is the unpalatable truth that the basic Gospel emphasis upon forgiveness has not yet become deeply rooted. The widespread fear of sorcery indicates a paucity of trust among neighbours, even within one's extended family. On the macro scale too, the differences between political parties are marked by such distrust and envy that erupts from time to time in acts of violence.

In Europe, it may be observed, witchcraft died out by the eighteenth century, or soon after. It coexisted with the Church therefore for at least 1500 years. In the end it reached obsolescence in the Age of Reason. Was this the result of theology, was it rational enlightenment, or was it a newfound tolerance? Will it be eradicated from Malawi by renewed vigour in the Churches, at present lacking any real willpower to challenge it? Or will it be the slow process of education that will deliver people from its paralysing grip? Will it, in other words, be a victory for Christian faith or will it be rational thinking that prevails?

At a time of great social change, there are understandable indications of a desire to hold on to old beliefs (and fears), and even the wish to canonise them. Martin Ott, a university lecturer here, comments:

> The reluctance to accept the changes of time and their unavoidable consequences has many variants. Criticism against modernisation is one of

them, another is the almost canonising approach of contemporary African theologians towards African Traditional Religions. Any romanticism towards the African past can be understood from a human point of view, but it is unacceptable when we look at the problems that have to be addressed.

I recently took most of our Anglican ordinands to the Catholic mission station at Mua, some distance south-west of Lake Malawi. Here, in the museums dedicated to Malawian customs and culture, is the fruit of one dedicated priest's lifelong research. The young priest who showed us round was equally committed to the need for inculturation. The emphasis is on a respectful approach to African traditions, with the recognition, however, that, like some aspects of European culture, there are flaws and failings. In discussion afterwards, I found our ordinands united in resisting several of the customs represented in the museum. They thought African styles of song, rhythm, dance, even art forms (although in my view these are unlikely to be much noticed by Malawian congregations), were to be welcomed into the liturgy; likewise certain traditional practices at the time of death and burial. The masks used in ritual dancing with their exaggerated and often frightening features were not, however, considered suitable for use within a Christian context. They reckoned that some of the underlying religious concepts diluted Christian beliefs such as the uniqueness of Christ and the ultimate efficacy of the cross.

Ott claims that, despite the fragmentation and disorientation that can accompany urbanisation, it can also be life-enhancing, with enriched opportunities and wider social contacts. The anthropologist Monica Wilson commented some thirty years ago: 'To seek return to smallness of scale is no cure for our present disorders. Can one have the close-knit warmth and emotional security of an isolated village without stifling individuality?' She argued that on the larger scale of urban life 'there are greater heights and depths than in an isolated, pre-literate society.' Ott therefore pleads for an urban inculturation of Christian faith, rather than one that clings to traditional tribal practices.

So the question arises: How far can Anglicanism adjust to urban life in Malawi? Christianity needs a cutting edge in such a context, to challenge the unquestioned assumptions of tribal culture. Perhaps the way forward lies in stronger provision of vivid and imaginative worship rivalling anything that African tradition can offer. In a nutshell: sacramentality, properly taught and practised, is the antidote to superstition. Through the awareness of God's grace operative in every aspect of life comes the recognition that in all our uncertainties and setbacks as well as in the blessings that enrich us there is only one Lord, who remains close to us both in sorrow and in rejoicing. In any new environment, therefore, appropriate expressions of sacramentality need to be developed. This is well understood in some of the flourishing African Initiated Churches (AICs).

Please pray for those who are caught up in the tensions of village life, and for those who struggle to find new identity and community in urban situations.

Inculturation at Mua
The scene, taken from an external mural at the mission museum,
is an adaptation of Gule Wamkulu, the 'great dance'.
Masked figures (here as antelopes) relive the creation myths.
The snake symbolises God, who brings new life on earth.

AFRICAN CHRISTIANITY
September 2000

'YOU MAY, AND YOU MUST, have an African Christianity.' Pope Paul VI urged this at the first Pan-African meeting of Roman Catholic Bishops held in Uganda in 1969. He was, of course, following the lead given in the second Vatican Council earlier in the same decade which stated 'The Catholic Church ... looks with sincere respect upon those ways of conduct and of life, those rules and teachings which, though differing in many particulars from what she holds and sets forth, nevertheless reflect a ray of that Truth which enlightens all men.' In the thirty years since then, inculturation, as it is now known, has been a major concern for African Christians.

For many, the mission churches emanating from Europe seemed not to respond very adequately, and so there are now thousands of African Initiated Churches which to a greater or lesser degree incorporate African beliefs and customs. There must surely be a new AIC springing up somewhere in Malawi practically every week. Not all are recognisably Christian, nor would they all pretend to be – the Church of the Ancestors in Malawi being explicitly non-Christian. But numerically they claim the allegiance of a significant proportion of the population, and so collectively are on a par with the mainstream Churches. Clearly they pose a challenge: what is the secret of their success? What are the needs that seem to be met more adequately by them rather than by (say) the Anglican Church?

In 1985, when I was working in Lesotho, I served as the secretary of a major consultation held at Rhodes University, Grahamstown on *The Future of Christianity in Southern Africa*. It was my particular task to summarise the conclusions that were reached, and they were certainly not what I had anticipated in a sub-continent ruled by an apartheid regime. Unbelievably, apartheid hardly gained a mention! Instead, there was unanimity that the nettle to be grasped most firmly by the churches was Africanisation.

Among the mainstream churches the Roman Catholics seemed further ahead than most, perhaps because of the greater resources at their disposal (Lumko Institute, then in the Transkei, springs to mind), but also because of a more flexible theological approach. Fr Kabasele Lumbala of DR Congo has recently published a fascinating account of liturgical experimentation, mainly in his own country, but with passing reference to several other parts of Africa as well (for example, he cites the Poor Clares at Lilongwe in Malawi). He admits that as yet it has met only with 'a modified tolerance' rather than full approval, which means that the process of reception is still underway.

Aylward Shorter, the distinguished White Father from East Africa, wisely pointed out over twenty years ago, that 'the most important thing that should be said about African Christianity is that it is Christian. It is not enough to be African.' For that matter, a similar comment might be made about Anglican or Catholic or Protestant versions of the faith: the crucial test is whether they are Christian or not.

Where Roman Catholics have engaged readily with the local culture, sometimes even overstepping the mark (as famously archbishop Milingo did with his charismatic ministry in Zambia), Anglicans have been generally more cautious. In Lesotho in the 1980s it was hard to wean the local congregations off their translated version of Hymns Ancient and Modern (Victorian edition!), and our experience last year at the United College of the Ascension in Birmingham was that African students often launched into yet another rendering of Amazing Grace. Such attachment to the cultural trappings of the 'mother' Church is perhaps understandable. The emerging Church in Africa still needs and values its links with the wider world, and may not always have the confidence to jettison too much of its inheritance. It should not be overlooked either that liturgical or musical change quite often calls upon financial resources that may simply not be available.

On the whole, therefore, the Alcuin/Grove booklet which reported a few years ago on Anglican Liturgical Inculturation in Africa makes fairly timid reading. Bishop Colin Buchanan reckoned that in the mid 1980s the only relevant rubrics to be found in revised liturgies of the whole Anglican Communion were the use of bells, drums and rattles in New Guinea, and a dignified bow at the Sharing of the Peace in Korea. There is clearly scope to engage with local idiom much further in many places.

Yet whereas it is one thing to incorporate indigenous styles of singing and dancing, of costume, gesture and ornament, into the sacred liturgy, it is obviously something different to introduce changes that touch more closely upon the heart of the Christian faith. Fr Shorter's warning has to be taken seriously – so here two rather different issues are offered by way of illustration.

The role of the ancestors: many an African, faced with an important decision to make, with a problem to be handled, with an illness to face, with a setback to overcome, will want the strength and support of his ancestors, perhaps to guide him or to intercede for him, or otherwise to act for the benefit of his family. He may visit the place of his ancestors' burial, or possibly a message will come from them at night in a dream. Sometimes he may realise an offence has been done to one of them, for which appeasement must now be made with a symbolic offering.

In these contexts the word 'ancestor' means not just any forebear, but one who has lived a worthy life, dying a natural death, who was blessed with offspring and was able to provide for them. Beyond death it is believed the ancestor is even richer in his desire and ability to help his kith and kin. He has been termed 'the living dead'. Furthermore, he is closer to God than those left on earth, and his supplication is therefore considered to be more effective. All this is part of the African's natural respect for those who are older and more senior. Thus, if a villager wants to request something of his village chief, he will not approach the chief directly, but via the entourage of elders, beginning with the most junior, who then pass the request on upwards.

'Honour thy father and thy mother' is one of those commandments Western society has almost forgotten, so it is good to be reminded in Africa of family bonds of respect and affection. The danger, though, is of treating ancestors as entirely akin to those Christian saints whom we venerate, and whose intercession we ask. When Jesus taught his disciples to pray, he gave them the Our Father, a simple and direct prayer which he shares with us in the power of the Spirit. Because we are God's children, we can speak to him directly, even though in our frailty we cannot always articulate what we need to say and so, relying on the Holy Spirit working within us. We turn to our Lord himself as our great high priest and to the saints who belong with us in Christ's body for their prayers. It is not true, however, that God is so utterly distant that the 'living dead' necessarily have to approach him on our behalf. In Christ he came close to us so that in Christ we can become close also to him. Further, however much we respect and admire our ancestors, we know that they themselves need further purging and purification before they are able to bear the full radiance of God's presence, and that therefore we need to continue praying for them. Ancestor 'veneration' should not blind the African Christian to our universal need of grace at all times and in every stage of our pilgrimage towards heaven.

The eucharistic elements: in 1993 over forty representatives of the Anglican Church in Africa met to consider liturgical inculturation. This Kanamai Consultation made the startling recommendation, 'Probably the time has come when local foods and drinks could be substituted for wafers and wine.' The Congolese Fr Lumbala (in the book previously mentioned, *Celebrating Jesus Christ in Africa*) pursues the argument enthusiastically, with a learned summary of historical circumstances when alternatives received official sanction. A Russian Synod, for example, permitted cherry wine in the late 16th century, and a hundred years later the Copts were using unfermented raisin juice. He makes the obvious point that wheat flour and grape wine cannot be universally produced, and can be extremely expensive if imported.

Does this mean, however, that the Scots must consecrate whisky, the Chinese tea, and the Eskimo melted snow? Christ's incarnation surely locates some essential Christian symbolism in the particular circumstances of his life and death. We cannot dispense with the fact that he was actually a man and that he was born a Jew; nor that his advent was discerned to be 'in the fullness of time' in accordance with God's providential plan. Bread and wine are not to be seen as accidental features of Christ's dispensation, but as central to our Christian identity and our sacramental unity. If they prove costly and scarce for some of our Christian brothers and sisters, is this not a spur to others to help them out? Millet bread and banana wine, or their local equivalents, represent a move towards congregationalism rather than inculturation. To emphasise the eucharist as a meal made of convenience foods detracts from that heavenly banquet Christ has ordained that we should share with him.

So proper inculturation requires discernment, to adapt and transform those elements of local practice that are compatible with Christianity, but also to reject those that are not. While some missionaries from Europe may have been harsh and sweeping in their condemnation of 'pagan' ways, it must be remembered that others have laboured hard to appreciate the value of what was already in place. The early Jesuits in China are the most striking example of the latter, but in Malawi some of the pioneers were kindred spirits. Archdeacon William Johnson served the UMCA for 52 years, and received an Oxford D.D. for his efforts to translate the Bible into local languages. He also strove after the simple life, endeavouring to live as Africans did themselves, never really accepting the cathedral culture of Likoma Island.

On the other hand, it was very necessary in Malawi for slavery to be ended, and for harsh treatment of widows to be tempered with kindness and sympathy. When a man died, his widow would sometimes be faced with seclusion and starvation for a week, or with other such demeaning treatment. Then, after a year, she might be ritually cleansed by having intercourse with her brother-in-law. Amazingly, it was only last November that President Muluzi, faced with the reality of wide-spread AIDS, decided to outlaw this latter practice, despite grumblings even from some educated Malawians.

It is not only in Central Africa, of course, that the Gospel sheds its light upon prevailing customs. There is for each Christian a personal challenge to examine within ourselves: of the weighty baggage we accumulate in life, how much is there of Christ – how much indeed truly reflects and serves the Gospel?

Please pray for discernment as African ways of responding to the Gospel emerge, and for the readiness of the wider Church to be enriched by them too.

LANGUAGE OF THE HEART
October 2000

THE PRESENT EUCHARISTIC LITURGY of the Anglican Church in Malawi dates from 1976. It reflects much that was learnt in the process of revision in the Church of England that led to the publication of the *Alternative Services Book* in 1980, although in one or two respects (e.g. the positioning of the Prayer of Humble Access) it anticipates changes made more recently in *Common Worship*. But here there is no head of steam for much further revision, apart from a desire for more African (and less English) modes of expression. An English bishop visiting Zomba in August thought it would be helpful to supply us with all the Common Worship material. It might indeed sit usefully on our library shelves, but I have yet to come across any Malawian priest clamouring for a similar proliferation of eucharistic prayers. In fact, if any such liturgical development were ever to be considered here, it could only get under way if funding for a few reams of paper, some bus fares and copious diesel fuel was first provided!

Perhaps in any case there is more to liturgy than theologically correct phraseology. W.A.Graham in *Beyond the Written Word* (Cambridge 1987) reminds us that in many cultures religious texts have purposes going beyond the communication of specific content. There is the 'sensual' dimension:

> I use this word to suggest that *seeing, hearing,* and *touching* in particular are essential elements in religious life as we observe it. They deserve greater attention than our bias in favour of the mental and emotional aspects typically allows.

He then refers to modes such as chant and 'unthinking' repetitious singing, artistic or dramatic representation, the pageantry of solemn procession, even the devout touching of holy objects:

> The discursive understanding ... is not the only access to meaning in the interaction of the faithful with the text. Because we invest most of our time and effort poring over precisely the linguistic meaning ... we are least prepared to

tackle the question of meaning when it seems to be divorced from, or at least independent of, the literal, word-by-word content.

John Barton, in his *Hulsean Lectures* (1990) at Cambridge, comments too on the way the Gospel is proclaimed at mass:

> In Catholic and Orthodox liturgy, the reading of the Gospel is attended with special ceremonies that emphasize the holiness of the 'message' it communicates ... [so that] in reading 'God's Word' in the presence of God, the community reaffirms its relationship with God. There is an analogy with what linguists call 'phatic communion', where we speak to someone else not in order to communicate information, ask questions, or give instructions, but simply *to 'service' our relationship with them.*

In the same vein there is Origen's well-known advice about the approach to texts that seem shrouded in obscurity. Where human understanding fails, we should not be deterred from reciting the words: the very act of doing so engages us with God's mystery. So too defenders of Prayer Book English, as also of the Latin Mass, insist that there is a sense of divine mystery and transcendence more important than the mere transfer of information in intelligible words. Other religions would bear similar testimony: Muslims in particular would speak of an inherent sacrality in the very recitation of the Qur'an. For them, the original Arabic sounds are an utterance from God, regardless of how far such speech is comprehended.

So, meaningful liturgical texts are only part of the picture. Other (and for some) deeper significance may be discovered in their use. Ritual can express what cannot be put into words, and can be instrumental in enabling fruitful changes in a person or in a community to take place. Thus, the movement for liturgical renewal has often attempted to make Christian worship less of a spectacle with onlookers and more of a celebration in which the congregation actively participates. If it has not always succeeded, it is not necessarily the inadequacy of the texts, but a tendency to limit participation to certain prayers or responses. *Non-verbal expression* is also needed, whether of posture or movement, of silence or symbol, because this can help us engage more powerfully with a God who exceeds the reach of our words. We should never forget that in his communication with us his eternal Word was expressed not in a book but in an incarnate person.

Here in Malawi the cry for inculturation is not primarily a matter of using different Chewa words, nor in patterning Christ after some mythical African role (although a research project carried out in 1992-95 and covering 30 African countries gathered well over two hundred possible alternative images for Christ, such as the Great Ancestor, the Protective Hero or the Chief Physician). At heart it is about the *non-verbal* element of worship. In the centuries before church buildings were cluttered with seats or pews, when there was visibly a sacred space for the liturgy to be performed, there was surely much greater physical engagement by the congregation, able to move freely as an integral part of the action. Fortunately many African churches are still relatively unencumbered with chairs or fixed benches, and therefore are far less restrictive than those European churches where personal comfort is preferred (if not always achieved). Where pews or padded seats tend to divide and fragment a congregation, permitting us only to stand or sit, and sometimes to kneel, in the African arena (whether inside or outside) there is freedom to express a much wider range of responses. Dancing (or any appropriate bodily expression) does not need to be confined to the aisles.

It is of course the unforced rhythms of movement and the drum that strike the visitor to an African church. African Christians do not have separate vocabularies for the sacred and the secular, as in the West. A church liturgy in England is usually *sui generis*, unlike any other experience the worshipper will encounter during his or her working week. And I emphasise here that the gap is not likely to be bridged by the attempt to use everyday language in formal devotions, because the vocabulary of worship needs to be far more holistic. For the African, the church is an extension of his home, and he is quite at home in church. It is a place to celebrate before God with one's neighbours, and to bring before God the life that people share with each other. As a Tumbukan proverb (from Northern Malawi) puts it, 'A person is a person because of neighbours' – a theme that necessarily recurs in these reports – which means that the church's worship too needs to embrace a 'neighbourly' dimension.

It is therefore not only dancing and clapping which the visitor encounters, but the expression of many personal and communal concerns within the liturgy. On a typical Sunday people will come forward requesting a special blessing as they face hurdles at home or at work; they will ask for prayers before hospital treatment or prior to an exam; wedding rings and treasured items of clothing will be blessed; thank-offerings will also be made for prayers answered, for injuries healed, and for good health restored. There is no carefully formulated priestly manual which lays out hierarchically sanctioned texts in which to respond. I pray as the Holy Spirit directs me – and in English because my Chichewa is limited. But although to some, especially to children, these are strange words, they know full well what is happening. The sign of the cross, or a hand laid on in benediction, speak with perfect clarity in a language of their own.

I conclude that liturgy is too important to be left to the liturgists. It is hard for any liturgy to come alive if the congregation is dead. There is a Swahili saying, 'The brotherhood of coconuts is a meeting in the cooking pot', which suggests the important truth of barriers between human beings being broken down as they come together before God in worship, ready to engage with him and with one another. Africans, to give one further example, certainly expect reconciliation between parties who are at odds with each other to be achieved prior to their receiving holy communion.

Kwezani mitima yanu ('Lift up your hearts') is the priest's invitation to his people. The response *Tiikweza kwa Ambuye* ('We lift them to the Lord') is a phrase simply said or sung, but in Africa its *plural* expression is not just a matter of words!

Please pray that we may learn to engage more fully in occasions of worship, binding us more closely to each other and to our Lord.

CHALLENGES AND CONSTRAINTS
November 2000

AS I WRITE, we are drawing to the end of the academic year, with diploma and degree exams being sat this week and next. This means a heavy load of marking of course, but I am making sure also that I see all of our Anglican ordinands personally before they depart, either for their parish placements or (in the case of four final year students) to await ordination to the diaconate during Advent.

The good news is that soon I shall be joined here by another Anglican priest, Fr Christopher Mwawa, who comes from St Peter's, Lilongwe. He will be living in the newly constructed house originally intended for us. We are happily installed in a college house, 20 minutes walk from the campus.

Over the year I have been able to assist in the development of seminars – indeed I now bear the grand title of Director of Research. Since Easter we have had two seminars each term, at which papers on contemporary issues have been read. BD students also attend, along with faculty members from St Peter's Catholic Seminary and the Department of Religious Studies at the University of Malawi (both located in Zomba). Perhaps in a year's time we shall be able to publish a collection of these papers, as we are particularly fortunate in having on campus the office of Kachere Press, who have an impressive list of publications by Malawian academics. These enable the African voice to be heard further afield as seldom happens otherwise, given the dearth of African publishing houses.

At times we really feel our minority position within this largely Presbyterian college. That is not to criticise other members of staff, with whom there are excellent relationships. But our goals and priorities can differ, which means that an Anglican ethos has to be cultivated in other ways. This applies particularly in liturgical matters. Morning prayers are shared together at half past seven each morning, preceded by half an hour for private meditation, and then our Anglican group meets separately in the late afternoon for the daily office. Again, there is constraint in the availability of modules for the diploma and degree courses. They have evolved ecumenically, with Catholic and Protestant input, theoretically leaving students with flexibility of choice. At a recent ZTC staff meeting, however, it was stated that all fourth year BD students must study liberation and feminist theology, with sacramental and liturgical study ruled out altogether for our Anglican students. There is no doubt as to the preference of the Malawian bishops, but any sacramental teaching will need to be undertaken in our separate Anglican meetings.

When I wrote earlier of the limitations of the college library I had not appreciated that nowhere in Malawi is there any bookshop where academic or even fairly serious books can be obtained. Times Bookshops are represented in the larger towns, but sell only stationery, newspapers and a limited range of popular fiction. The churches set up a few bookshops of their own, but – apart from the shop attached to the Catholic church in Balaka, home of the Montfort Press – these are stocked entirely with rather tired 1950s and 1960s devotional tracts of a broadly evangelical persuasion, many of which have been donated by ministers in England on finding themselves with less available shelf space in their retirement. Under Dr Banda's regime the Malawi Book Service flourished and sold good non-fiction and academic works, but only because of its monopoly on the sale of school textbooks. After the 1994 elections this monopoly ended and with it the MBS itself. It is sad for Malawi that even those few who have sufficient money to buy books cannot stretch their minds or be in touch with modern thought, except by ordering special imports. I enquired through Church House Bookshop in London as to the likely cost of sending just a paperback to Malawi. The figure suggested was around £9-10, perhaps doubling the price of the book. Can you begin to imagine what it is like to live in a country where there are virtually no books or only a few (possibly outdated) second-hand ones?

This situation affects our teaching in more than one way. Where there is only one available book on a given subject, it is treated with undue reverence. My classes are constantly rather shocked when I suggest that the author may have got it wrong, and that they should use their own critical faculties. In biblical studies in particular I emphasise that the conclusion is only as strong as the evidence supporting it, so students should not treat their commentaries as final dogmatic authorities. But it is not easy for any society that has been under totalitarian rule for 30 years, as was Malawi under Dr Banda, to learn to debate and to discuss freely and to weigh the strength of different arguments.

The mission task here is as much about empowerment – undermining the dependency culture – as anything else. We had a visit in August from the Moderator of the Church of Scotland, as part of the 125th anniversary celebration of the Scottish mission here. One of his observations was that CCAP (the Presbyterian Church) was still in many ways living as it did 125 years ago. 'We have changed in Scotland,' he said, 'but you are still practising as we once taught you long ago.' Change comes slowly here in the churches' response to present-day Malawi. Some hold fast to the belief that real religion was taught by white men in the 1880s and 1890s, and that not only is scripture and doctrine to be held sacred but so too are the details of church practice and administration.

This applies in particular to the hymns that form the bulk of our college repertoire, which are mostly translations from the revivalist collections made by I. D. Sankey in late 19th century America. The believer is usually depicted in them on a mountain side, in a barren desert, in a dark and gloomy storm, or caught at sea in a tempest – clichés that begin to seem threadbare with over-use, and unable to connect adequately with real-life issues such as AIDS and other diseases, corruption, sorcery, unemployment, family dislocation, and a bleeding environment. Specific cross-references may well be too narrow and have too limited a shelf life, but it should be easier for a worshipper to celebrate in song something of the biblical vision of God's grace raising humanity from the depths of suffering and privation in a way that resonates with the contemporary world. Secular songs in Malawi seem to reflect public needs and feelings well ahead of the churches.

It is the Catholic Church that has responded fastest to the issue of inculturation, while CCAP remains strongly resistant. Anglicans (as one might expect) are somewhere in the middle. Although worship at St George's, Zomba can be a little staid, out in the villages worship pulses to the beat of many drums and the mass comes alive with rhythm and dancing. On our last rural expedition, a two hour trek from Zomba, I danced from Chimbeta's mud and thatch church through the adjacent field of stubble back to our truck, followed by the entire congregation of about ninety people who came to bid us farewell. Urban congregations by contrast are now just as likely to throb to electronic keyboards and guitars.

One aspect of dependency that dies hard is the financial scene. Our college is supported almost entirely by overseas grants from partner churches or from mission organisations. We are very grateful, yet I calculated that, at least as regards the Anglican contribution, if every adult church member in Malawi gave the equivalent of half a penny each week, our quota would easily be exceeded. We have 22 ordinands at present, costing 50,000 kwacha (£500) each per annum to the Anglican Church here. If only clergy taught the principles and practice of stewardship, the church in Malawi could be much more nearly self-supporting. Many people are poor, but collectively they are richer than they realise. It must surely be imperative in the coming years, despite all the many problems, for Malawians to be given the confidence to achieve things on their own.

One consequence of the present arrangements is that our Principal, Dr Mwakanandi, is on the telephone almost every day, begging for funds to run the college. These funds have usually already reached Malawi from donor churches, but on arrival have been 'temporarily diverted' to meet other needs. In other words, the diocese or synod which acts as the financial intermediary has decided to prioritise other projects (such as clergy pay) above ZTC, which has to wait its turn before receiving its (theoretically ring-fenced) allocation.

As we take more students into the degree programme the pressures will increase, since their funding will need to be extended by an extra year. One very urgent task is to find extra accommodation for them as well before next January. There is a lot of pressure on us *azungus* ('white men') to use our influence back home. We are caught between urgent short term imperatives and the longer term need for Christians in Malawi to discover their own God-given resources.

Please pray for Dr Mkakanandi, for better understanding between the churches of their different traditions, and for empowerment of Malawian Christians.

PUTTING DOWN ROOTS
December 2000

AFTER LIVING OUT OF SUITCASES for the first three months, it was a great relief to get properly settled just before Easter. A lot of repairs had to be effected around the house (inherited from a previous lecturer), mostly minor works such as replacing broken windows or rusting mosquito gauze. The garden needed attention too, but now we have a thriving vegetable patch to accompany the banana, mango and paw-paw trees. Already we are eating our own carrots, lettuce, tomatoes, turnips and spinach.

Our household has also expanded to include Carolyn, a Malawian girl who was orphaned 10 years ago, and is living with us as she prepares to take her school certificate examinations. If she passes, she hopes to train as a nurse at St Luke's Hospital, Malosa. We are also able to support several local families who help in different ways. Not long ever seems to pass before another of them has some medical emergency or a further bereavement. They seem to regard us as particularly generous by local standards, but the reality is that their hourly rate is at most the equivalent of fifteen pence – plus one good daily meal. With Asian traders, we gather, the rate is roughly one-third of this, which certainly attracts public protests from time to time. These figures may be compared with the earnings of the teaching staff at college, most of whom have doctorates, on a monthly income of around £100. Yet supermarket prices are much the same as in England, the saving grace being that many Africans can grow their own maize and vegetables, which in any case are relatively cheap to buy in the market. The only item conspicuously lower in price from the UK is meat, which is affordable to us if not to the beggars waiting outside each shop.

Then there is Duncan, who calls every morning for his breakfast but acts as our recycling agent. He collects our used packets and papers which, together with any empty bottles, he sells in Zomba market. He was once most indignant when we inadvertently referred to these as our 'rubbish': for him they are valuable raw materials. There is a use for everything in this country, which in that respect is far less wasteful than the Western way of life. Unfortunately, as Duncan is getting older, he suffers from high blood pressure and was in hospital recently.

Every day people knock on our door, some with a pitiful tale of unfed children. Not all of them are quite genuine. Last week a man made his way painfully up our path, and then lowered himself with every sign of exhaustion into the chair on our veranda. He had not eaten, he said, for three days, and needed to get to Blantyre for an operation on his heart. We offered him a substantial loaf of bread, together with a cup of water and a mango – but no cash. He took one bite from the mango and then left it, and when he discovered that money was not on offer, snatched up the loaf without a word of thanks, making off hastily, looking very much more agile and fit than our first impression of him.

Since we have a vehicle of our own, people often look to us for help with transport. We have taken ordinands and their wives on several visits, ferried Mothers' Union (MU) members from St George's and on one occasion collected a coffin. The deceased turned out to be a giant at six foot nine inches and it was fascinating to watch how the joiner extended a standard box by another 18 inches. Back in the home village the gratitude was immense but the mourners' wailing was unforgettable. One key difference, so we have learnt, between a Christian funeral and that of a Muslim is the involvement of the whole community, including *women*, in the former.This has sometimes contributed to the conversion of some Muslim women.

Links with the local MU have been very interesting. On Sarah's very first visit there, many had arrived ahead of time, and were sitting on the grass enjoying long sticks of sugar cane. Having stripped off the outer skin with their teeth, they sucked out the sweet juice and spat the remaining inedible pulp onto the ground around them. Quite a different spectacle from an English MU gathering! Earlier this year they were preparing for their 80th anniversary celebrations, held at the end of August on church grounds near Mangochi. All participants had a specially designed *chitenje* for the festival, made into a costume by a tailor in the market. Bishop Peter of Lake Malawi presided at the vast open air mass, while our own bishop James preached. The occasion was graced by the President of Malawi himself, who arrived to great excitement in a helicopter (and a cloud of dust). The MU members had learnt the songs and dances which were performed and in his concluding speech President Muluzi, a Muslim, spoke of religious freedom for all in Malawi. Now the big event is over, our local MU is focusing on how to respond further to the AIDS epidemic.

On several Sundays we have ventured into the remoter villages, on bumpy dirt roads. On one such occasion we had to plunge through the river where a bridge had collapsed. Because each parish covers a wide geographical area, 20 to 30 outstations are not uncommon – yet this means that a visit from a priest is none too frequent and each congregation has to rely strongly on lay leaders. In one church we found nearly three dozen women waiting to be enrolled as MU members, with several lay readers in line to be given their bishop's licence and several Muslims preparing to be received as Christians. In another place there were 15 babies waiting to be christened at the end of mass. So we see the Anglican Church flourishing and continuing to expand in many ways. It is a privilege to worship with such welcoming and warm-hearted people, and positively overwhelming when they once sent us on our way with all sorts of gifts – cabbages, sweet potatoes, cassava, eggs and three live chickens. Knowing how little they have, it was humbling to see such generosity.

We have made good friends at St George's and at the college, where there is a supportive community of staff and their wives. We were happy to have our daughter Patricia here with a friend during their university summer break. Together we discovered a little of Lake Malawi and saw elephants, crocodiles, hippos and beautiful birds in Liwonde National Park. We look forward to seeing our son and daughter-in-law for Christmas.

Up on Zomba plateau we are also fortunate in having a network of paths to explore – along by the Mulunguzi river (which is now filling the new dam), through the forested areas, right to the edge of the escarpment where magnificent views open up. One day we had a local lad with the intriguing name of Assam Whiskey as our guide to the top of the highest peak (about 7000 feet). He speaks fluent English and Chewa, but like many people in this region was born in Mozambique and took refuge here in the 1980's. He is a Yao (like Malawi's President Muluzi) and therefore a Muslim. His mother was shot dead by soldiers when he was two, but his father survived and is a carpenter. At the age of 18 he still attends primary school, but has little hope of progressing further since secondary schooling costs too much money. Like many Malawians he is enterprising and offered us extra-special prices on his father's carvings – even so, it causes a pang of conscience to succumb to such bargains, when one realises that at home such exquisite and imaginative craftsmanship could command perhaps forty or fifty times as much. If only Malawi had access (as for example Kenya does) to adequate and inexpensive air freight.

Last week we took four days off to walk on the Mulanje massif, 40 miles from here. To get back to base we had a ride in a broken-down truck with a crazed windscreen, bald tyres, wobbly steering, a flat battery and a seriously leaking radiator. That is how many locals get around, so we feel we're almost Malawian now. Of course, very few own a car or other vehicle, although low-priced Chinese bicycles are increasingly in evidence. Regular maintenance or repair of any equipment, however, is often beyond people's means.

Not so long ago we needed a replacement for the rear window of our truck, which was broken on our way back from a women's cooperative in a village near the Shire river. We had bought some bamboo chairs from them, which (curiously) were based on a picture torn out from an old *Country Living* magazine. We had almost reached home when the truck jolted after hitting an unsuspected pothole in the road. A few days later we went into Blantyre to the glass works, but actually opted for Perspex rather than glass. The factory floor was covered with shards of broken glass, and the manager remarked that 'accidents occur here every day'. The fitter had himself lost half his fingers in the twenty years he had worked there – and received no compensation. For him, it was a job worth keeping regardless. Life, as all our readers must now realise, is so very different here.

Thank you so much for your continuing support. We pray God's blessings upon you this Christmas, and for his strength and guidance in the year ahead.

Please pray for lay leaders in remote churches, where a visit from a priest is infrequent, and for those who have assumed responsibility for the care of orphans.

YEAR 2001

Pel's Fishing Owl
As seen early one morning high in a tree at Liwonde.
These birds are very large and not at all common.

Pounding maize
The women lifting their heavy pestles
sing to keep up a steady rhythm
(e.g. 'the one who gives up first is married to a frog').
Only the few with any money will use a maize mill instead.

THE ROLE OF REPETITION
January 2001

I AM NO GREAT LINGUIST, despite long years at school learning French and Latin, and then some German. Later on I picked up enough New Testament Greek to bluff my way through Theology Schools at Oxford, and enough Sesotho to say Mass in Lesotho – although my downfall always came after the service when people tried to engage me in conversation. I certainly don't pretend as did an early American evangelist to a Pentecostal gift of tongues, on the strength of which he sailed for Calcutta, addressed the natives in what he imagined was Bengali, but was so upset when they couldn't understand a word he spoke that he sailed straight back home again.

There is of course much more to communication than simply knowing the words. Body language can cover a multitude of ignorance, and gutteral noises such as *'ee'* uttered with convincing gestures can speak volumes. Actually I once travelled round France with a friend who had but a single phrase in his repertoire, *'comme ça'*, which - accompanied by hand signals - nevertheless seemed entirely adequate for most purposes. My friend was generally more successful in making his needs known than I was with my richer O level vocabulary!

English, somewhat to my relief, is the official language of Malawi, although since independence most people speak the tribal language Chichewa as promoted by Dr Banda. Chichewa is actually spoken by up to 15 million people throughout Central Africa, and is probably the most common Bantu language there. Attempts to practise it, however, are frequently frustrated by Malawians insisting that they need to practise their English! Before coming to Malawi we already knew a little Chewa through attendance at the Africa Centre near Covent Garden. Our tutor was a Malawian lady whose husband was on the High Commission staff. We became proficient in saying Hello and Goodbye, as well as in offering tea, with or without milk and/or sugar!

She also introduced us to the world of African idiom. Through it I came to my surprise to appreciate a little more about the idiom of the

Bible, and something about the way we use words in liturgy, and indeed about the very role of liturgy in bridging the gulf that separates man from God. There is a common link, as I discovered, in the use of repetition to emphasise or to intensify meaning.

Let me first illustrate this with a few Chichewa expressions. *Kamodzi* on its own means 'once', but repeated in the word *kamodzikamodzi* it takes on the sense of 'once in awhile' or 'very occasionally'. The verb-stem -*wala* has the root meaning 'shine' whereas the double *waliwali* indicates something that is 'flashing'. Other ideophones include *balalabalala* ('swarming'), *dzidzidzi* ('suddenly'), *nda nda nda* ('in a line'), *peku-peku* ('all agog'), *vwevwe* ('full to bursting'), *zwezwe* ('vanished'). It is not that words expressing a superlative are unknown to the language (e.g. *kwabasi* means 'extremely') but that a repetition enables the speaker to project him or herself more emphatically into what is being said.

Hence when some Africans are talking in English about, say, the weather, it does not now surprise me if they say 'It's cold-cold today' rather than 'It's very cold'; or 'I'm so happy-happy-happy' instead of 'I'm feeling extremely happy'. The usage points not to inadequate command of English so much as to an idiomatic way of stressing a point.

And indeed, this is not confined to the African. I know but a little Hebrew (although I have always been aware of the parallelism in the Psalms), but Hebraists tell me that repetition is also a Semitic characteristic. One of the best examples is the triple 'Holy, holy, holy' of Isaiah 6.3 which becomes the Tersanctus of the Eucharistic Prayer. It is not vain repetition, but an expression of the utterly surpassing holiness of God. One epithet 'holy' is by itself quite inadequate, because a transcendental quality needs to be brought out, as we might elsewhere suggest in the phrase 'holy of holies'. Many other scriptural examples of threefold repetition can readily be cited that emphasise an expression or intensify the meaning of a word. The threefold formula of blessing proposed to Aaron and his sons is the strongest possible affirmation of God's favour (Num 6.22–27). Its nearest equivalent in Christian writing is perhaps Paul's benediction, 'The grace of the Lord Jesus Christ and the love of God and the fellowship of the Holy Spirit be with you all' (2 Cor 13.14). Again, the depth of the psalmist's distress is conveyed in his prayer 'evening and morning and at noon' (Ps 51.17). Likeness Daniel's resilient faith is expressed in the petition he makes to God 'three times a day' (Dan 6.13).

With this in mind, we can turn to other liturgical uses. Early in the mass the *Kyries* are said or sung, or become part of a more extensive litany. Here it is not simply a matter of reiteration, nor of variants upon a theme. Each succeeding *Kyrie eleison* takes us deeper into the compassionate heart of our Lord, and as we plumb the depths of our own shortcomings so we learn to cast ourselves more unreservedly upon the undeserved goodness and mercy of our loving Saviour.

In the Orthodox tradition, the Jesus prayer has a similar character. It is said, not once, not a hundred times, but thousands upon thousands of times until it becomes part of the rhythm of thinking and of breathing, immersing the supplicant in the very being of Christ. Praying the Rosary has something of the same import for Catholics. Last year, Father Timothy Radcliffe, Master of the Dominican Order, wrote in *Priests and People*:

> Many religions are marked by this tradition of the repetition of sacred words ... I heard a Buddhist service, and it seemed to consist in the endless repetition of holy words, the mantra. It has often been pointed out that the rosary is quite similar to these Eastern ways of prayer, and that the constant reiteration of these words can work a slow but deep transformation of our hearts.

He cited G. K. Chesterton, who argued that repetition is a characteristic of the vitality of children, who like the same stories, with the same words, time and time again, not because they are bored and unimaginative, but because they delight in life. In the same way, one can imagine that God says every morning 'Do it again' to the sun; and every evening 'Do it again' to the moon. The repetition in nature need not be seen as mere recurrence; it may be more of a theatrical encore!

Awareness of repetition as a typical African idiom gives rise to the frequent criticism of Western liturgies that they appear to value doctrinal correctness and what the Vatican 2 document *Sacrosanctum Concilium* described as 'noble simplicity' far more than any emotional engagement of the people. In African culture, words communicate feelings, which are strengthened by repetition. Ethiopia, for example, has several Eucharistic prayers of considerable antiquity whose reverberating poetic form is far from 'simple'. In recent times (1989) Catholic bishops in West Africa have asserted that Africa's cultural affinities are much more with the Jewish roots of Christianity than with its subsequent Greco-Roman developments.

In England I suspect that many of those who love and use *The Book of Common Prayer* do so, not out of any exaggerated devotion to Elizabethan prose, nor because they cannot see any shortcomings of that book, but because, known by heart through regular repetition, it is possible to enter more deeply into the familiar words and to pray not only with the lips but with the spirit also. Familiarity breeds here, I think, not contempt, but a heightened awareness of the sacred. Ministering not only to the relatively illiterate but also to those nearing the end of their lives (whether in England because of advanced age, or in Malawi because of AIDS) the liturgy that serves best in extremity is surely again one that is embedded in the memory, rather than extracted from a text. If words are seldom repeated and liturgies are disposable, what help is afforded otherwise to those who lack the strength or the ability to read any more? Of course, this is not an argument for repetitious forms that are unduly verbose or riddled with opaque language: Jesus, after all, condemned the heaping up of 'empty phrases' (Matt 6.7). Rather, it is a needful reminder from African usage that some words or phrases may have a resonance that deepens with repetition, and can transport us as we pray them.

Please pray the Our Father several times each day in solidarity with fellow believers around the world.

LOOKING AHEAD
February 2001

THE ACADEMIC YEAR in Zomba closed in October and reopened at the beginning of January. The first thing we did in the break was to take a short holiday. We sailed on the Ilala as it made its weekly journey up and down Lake Malawi, dropping off passengers and all sorts of cargo, including live hens, sacks of maize and bicycles, at a dozen or so little villages on the shore. At one point we even loaded up with 89 tonnes of sugar and crossed the lake to the Tanzanian village of Mbamba Bay, where it took half a day to get the bags ashore using the two ship's boats – packed by the crew each time to far more than their safe capacity. The ship's engineer had declined to make the crossing at all as he considered we were overladen, but fortunately the weather remained calm and the lake was placid. We were unable to set foot on the Tanzanian side and to walk on the beach as the immigration official demanded 50 US dollars apiece for the privilege, so we spent the day on deck catching a pleasant breeze while taking in the panorama of tall palm trees bordering the golden sands. Coming back south we anchored off Likoma Island and were fortunate in finding the dean, who gave us a guided tour of St Peter's Cathedral (nearly as large as Winchester). He explained that its high altar was positioned by Chauncy Maples so as to stand on the exact spot where he had witnessed the burning of a witch.

Once back home, it was down to the business of preparing talks and lectures, first for the annual clergy retreat at Chilema (adjacent to the diocesan headquarters at Malosa) in November. This lasted three full days and was my first opportunity to meet the priests serving in Southern Malawi. We proceeded on the Sunday to the ordination service, where bishop James was assisted by two of the Zambian bishops, archbishop Bernard of Central Africa and bishop Leonard, both of them Malawians. It was particularly good to renew our acquaintance with archbishop Bernard, who came to our Somerset parish some years ago as part of a diocesan link. The ordination (two priests and three deacons) was a wonderful service, lasting some five hours. It was televised, with highlights broadcast later on two separate occasions on Malawian television.

My chief remaining task before Christmas was to write an ethics handbook for our third year course, having discovered the inadequacy of the existing textbook and the paucity of moral theology in the library. Fortunately the local Montfort Press publish an excellent bimonthly magazine *The Lamp* which deals with current political, social, economic and religious issues, and so provides plenty of material with which to bring ethical questions alive for the students.

I have been given two further biblical courses for this year: Pauline studies for the diploma course and Johannine studies for the BD students. So, along with teaching the synoptic gospels and Acts to our new first year students and continuing our exploration of Anglicanism in the afternoons, I find myself fully occupied. One member of staff retired back to Northern Ireland last year, but it seems likely that another expatriate may be joining us soon from Scotland. This is very necessary as the college continues to expand. I rejoice in a further Anglican colleague now, Fr Christopher Mwawa, who has come from Lilongwe. Shortly, therefore, we will have ten full-time staff, together with part-time specialists in Hebrew, Greek, music, and development studies.

Expansion does of course bring problems of its own. The most pressing difficulty, as highlighted previously, is the provision of sufficient accommodation for our extra students (and their families if they have them). For this academic year it has proved necessary for all new students to leave their families behind in their home villages. This situation is much regretted, especially as it affects ordinands whose homes are far away – in the far north of Malawi or even further afield in Zambia or Zimbabwe. The cost of travel prohibits most of these men from seeing their families more than once or twice during the course of the year. Fortunately, partner churches have begun to respond to our appeals and money has been promised from the United States and from Holland towards the new student housing.

The anticipated Anglican development may, it seems, be going ahead by the middle of this year. As described previously, the site is further down Chirunga Road towards the university. It is owned by the Anglican

Church, but is still occupied temporarily despite the completion of the Mulunguzi dam (which is already full to overflowing). A firm of engineers, subcontracted to complete the upgrading of Zomba's water piping, is now using the site as their depot. When their work is completed, there are plans to convert the buildings and offices into small housing units, and even to add some extra ones. Money for this, I am pleased to say, has come from my old college in Cambridge, St John's. It was the students there, prompted by the chaplain and the dean, who resolved to use their fund for education in Southern Africa to support us. So a generous grant of £25,000 has already been sent. I understand too that negotiations are underway with USPG for a history graduate to spend some time with us later this year.

I note that there is a tendency for developments of this sort to be placed almost entirely in the hands of the clergy here in Malawi, when in fact there are competent and qualified lay people to do much of the work. I am pressing for a theology of the laity to be studied and put into practice. It is amazing that even in college, when financial matters are discussed, the treasurer, who is a layman, is not invited to the meeting. It is, however, to the credit of the Anglican Church that some of Malawi's outstanding political and civic leaders have come from her ranks. The most moving, spiritually incisive address on AIDS that I have heard so far was given by an Anglican layman, Vice-President Justin Malewezi.

On a more personal note, I must thank several friends in the supporting parishes for sending out books to read. They are most appreciated, and certainly get a good circulation among friends in Zomba as well. Christmas cards arrived here in the end, even if towards the end of January. Postal services remain sluggish and unreliable. One parcel arrived here recently after a leisurely journey lasting three years. I investigated the parcel depot in Limbe (near Blantyre) last month, and discovered a huge hall with a mountain of mail-bags – and no one working there. When I wrote to the official in charge, suggesting as mildly as I could that the system might be improved, he replied very apologetically. His letter took three weeks to reach me from Blantyre, a distance of about 40 miles. In former times there was an overnight service, when runners from each end would exchange sacks at a halfway point. The office where they met and rested before setting off back is now a small museum.

However, email is a great boon for keeping in touch. I bought our first-ever computer last year from a South Korean Presbyterian colleague who was preparing to move on to missionary work in Moscow. Its modem blew one day in the aftermath of a thunderstorm; I gather that the voltage on the telephone line had jumped up well beyond its usual bounds. Fortunately there are several excellent IT firms in Blantyre, staffed by extremely competent Indians. Another technological advance here is the steady advance of mobile phone networks to cover most of the country. Soon we shall also have a new FM transmitter in Blantyre, enabling us to get easier reception of the BBC World Service (the problem with short wave being the need to switch frequencies at different times of the day, and even then to find considerable background interference). Zomba is of course privileged in having access to mains electricity, unlike 95% of the country, although such access is restricted by frequent power cuts and the occasional stealing of power lines. Small scale solar power units are beginning to be seen occasionally, and our diocese hopes to introduce them gradually into its rural rectories.

Looking down in the evening on Zomba town from the plateau above, all that is visible are a few lights here and there. Otherwise it is bathed in darkness. The 50,000 or more inhabitants for the most part use lamps before retiring early to bed. They then rise with the sun. This sounds a healthy lifestyle, but it scarcely promotes a 'wealthy and wise' population – by which I mean that, because of inadequate lighting at home in the evenings, children are unable to do much homework or reading before returning to school the next day. But then they are unlikely to have any books to read either – so I begin to understand how the circle of deprivation operates. Little time to read (because of the many chores to be done) coupled with poor conditions in which to do so restricts literacy and the demand for reading material.

Please pray for schools in Malawi, especially for our Anglican secondary school at Malosa next to diocesan headquarters.

LIFE IN THE RAW
March 2001

IT WAS WELL OVER a year ago when we left England for Malawi. What seemed so strange at first is now so familiar, although we are constantly learning much about the people here and their country. The rains started in good time and have been plentiful, hence all around Zomba it looks very green. The maize is flourishing wherever fertiliser has been used, but is rather sad and stunted elsewhere. We've recently been besieged by requests for loans to buy fertiliser, which is unaffordable to at least two-thirds of Malawians. More recently we've also been asked to help with school fees (few Malawians have any savings).

Sarah has continued to keep her links with the local Mothers' Union (MU). They are a lively group, constantly involved with the range of social problems that affect families. Many of the members are from nearby villages, and from time to time groups of members walk out to visit the sick and bereaved even there, outside Zomba.

Many initiatives have been set up by the MU to help deal with the ever-increasing problem of orphans (the inevitable offshoot of the AIDS pandemic). Currently, MU members are surveying Zomba and its surrounds to assess the numbers and situation of orphans, hence to see how best help can be given. As far as possible, orphans are looked after by their extended families and kept in their own villages. But, as the MU members report from their first-hand experience, the going is hard when people are so often unemployed and there are extra mouths to feed. There is also the problem of elderly grandparents trying to look after grandchildren when they themselves need looking after too.

Other areas of social concern include the local hospital and the prison in Zomba. Each of these establishments has to cope with appalling conditions. The MU will be making one of their regular prison visits shortly, taking basic requirements for the prisoners, such as soap and toothpaste. Similarly, it is only when the MU helps out in the hospital wards that they get a thorough clean. Otherwise there is an almost complete absence of cleaning materials. There is also only one consultant in Zomba hospital at present. Previous doctors have left after only a few months, being unable to keep going in such depleted circumstances. Being a state-run hospital means there are never any reserve funds for medication and nurses are grossly underpaid. In fact, they do not stay long either if they can get a job elsewhere, for example in a clinic that has some overseas funding. Consequently there is a severe shortage of nursing staff in Zomba itself. Our nearest neighbour was until recently a nurse at St Luke's Hospital, Malosa, but has given up her job for the time being because the pay barely covers the minibus fare there and back each day.

Eighty per cent of the patients have AIDS-related illnesses and wards are usually full to overflowing. Often there are two patients to a bed, or otherwise on the floor, or even under the bed – possibly without a mat to lie on. The situation is particularly bad just now because of the heavy rains. Whatever climate change may mean in other parts of the world, its impact here seems to be in terms of unpredictability. Although the overall annual rainfall does not vary hugely, it seems to fall more erratically than in the past, so that the chances of either drought or deluge have increased. At present we are faced with the latter problem. Mud and grass huts have collapsed and pit latrines in some of the villages are overflowing. This has led to a serious outbreak of cholera, with over 600 deaths throughout the country (representing about four per cent of those believed to have been infected). A similar crisis occurred only a few months ago as well, and was then accompanied by the spread of meningitis. We have learnt this through some of the nurses at St George's Church, as well as through Sarah's MU visits. The nurses are very dedicated people, although often run off their feet.

When our son Gabriel and his wife stayed with us for three weeks over Christmas, they brought about twenty teddy bears that they wanted to donate to the children's ward in hospital. However, they were speechless when they saw the babies lying on the floor in the intensive care ward and so many malnourished babies and children. When first visiting some months ago, Sarah noticed how many children seemed just to be staring into space with nothing to do. So now she has started to go in with constructive and creative things for them to do, especially for the children who are there with broken limbs or burns. Her main inadequacy is language. This gives a real incentive to improve her Chichewa, even though artwork enables the children to pick up a great deal simply by watching and imitating. At home, therefore, Carolyn has been an enormous on-going help in teaching her phrases and sentences to use with the children, who – coming mainly from the villages – know little or no English.

In college, we are developing good links with the Anglican ordinands and their families. We continue to have groups of them to our house, often on a Wednesday after our Eucharist. Last week, three of the newest ordinands came and told us how concerned they were that so many of their contemporaries at school had died of AIDS. HIV/AIDS really does seem to hit people in the 15 to 25 age group most of all, making future prospects both in the villages and in all areas of development look very daunting.

Sarah has recently been asked whether she would be able to teach some of the ordinands' wives how to sew and to use the hand-sewing machines. The college has six of these, none of which, she discovered, worked properly. After some cleaning, oiling and adjustments, three are now functioning quite well, so a programme can now be planned. Many clergy wives are keen to learn some craft or skill (such as sewing) that will bring in a little extra money to help feed the orphans they take in. It is hard to do this on the meagre clergy salaries alone.

New restrictions were recently necessary in college when it was discovered that several of the 2nd and 3rd year ordinands were each keeping around twenty or thirty chickens, not outside, but actually *inside* their small houses. One of the problems of keeping chickens here at all is the current rat infestation. Some education is needed about the disposal of kitchen waste such as uneaten *nsima* ('cooked maizemeal'), which tends to be discarded on a garden heap, subsequently attracting rodents.

It was so good to have our family with us over Christmas, and we had a lovely time with them and with friends. We had the opportunity to relax, visiting Lake Malawi and a couple of game reserves.* We are particularly fascinated by the wild life here. Our daughter gave Sarah a pair of binoculars which she finds invaluable. We have seen such a variety of wonderful birds in their breeding plumage, including several different kingfishers and a beautiful owl, known as a Pel's fishing owl. Our favourite garden bird is the Heuglin's robin, especially for the amazing variety of his song. It saddens us to know that not far away in the direction of Lake Chilwa hundreds of birds (seed-eaters known as queleas) flock to feed in the rice paddy fields, but are caught in huge nets – 50 to 100 at a time – only to be sold in the local markets for a kwacha or two each. Imagine rows of them there impaled on sticks. Thousands of birds are killed like this each year in Malawi, yet another example of how wildlife faces a real threat here. Of course, the underlying cause is the continuing human poverty.

We ended the year 2000 by celebrating Carolyn's 21st birthday with a special meal just after Christmas. Carolyn, the orphan who lives with us, has finished school now, and awaits the results of her Malawi school certificate exams. No doubt 2001 will open new doors for her, as for all of us.

Please pray for Carolyn and for the many other orphans – and for the relatives and villagers who care for them.

---

*   Liwonde National Park is just over an hour's drive away and borders the Shire river. During a 24 hour stay there in December, we saw the following birds — apart of course from lots of other lovely plants and creatures:

Pygmy kingfisher	*Red bishop bird*	*Masked weaver*
African jacana	*Wattled plover*	*Striped kingfisher*
Brown-hooded kingfisher	*Lilac-breasted roller*	*Little bee eater*
Crowned hornbill	*Burchell's coucal*	*Woodland kingfisher*
Lesser blackwinged plover	*White backed night heron*	*Barred owl*
Mozambique nightjars	*Hadeda ibis*	*Striped cuckoo*
Squacco heron	*Redbilled fire finches*	*Tropical boubou*
Western banded snake eagle	*Blue waxbill*	*Böhms bee eater*
White browed sparrow weavers	*Pied kingfisher*	*Kittlitz's plover*
Collared palm thrush	*Malachite kingfisher*	

PROVERBIAL SAYINGS
April 2001

PROVERBS, even wisecracks, play a more important part in African cultures than in Europe. Many of the minibuses that ply their trade carry a message to the public, blazoned in front or behind. 'God help us' and 'Things fall apart' are two slogans often seen in the Zomba area, somehow failing to inspire complete confidence in the vehicle's roadworthiness. More innocuously there is a small fleet which reads 'The way it comes' as it approaches, and 'The way it goes' as it retreats. Shop fronts are often labelled in the same fashion. The 'No money no friends' maize mill makes its point succinctly to the ever hopeful cash-strapped customer. Slightly more puzzling was the notice seen recently by a friend outside a restaurant, 'You're not going to be happy'. He asked the proprietor if this was not rather off-putting for a potential diner? 'Not at all,' was the reply, 'It's not for those eating here already. We're telling people standing outside that they're really missing a great treat. They're not going to be happy until they come in and join us.' So, as Professor George Caird used to reiterate endlessly in our biblical lectures at Oxford, 'meaning is text plus context'. To *azungus* ('strangers') the African context is not always what it seems.

In Chichewa, proverbs are called *mwambi*. The term includes riddles and other oral genres which not only reflect the African world-view but also express the practical wisdom of society. Bishop Patrick Kalilombe (now at the University in Zomba but previously a lecturer whom we knew in Selly Oak, Birmingham) describes Malawian proverbs in these words:

> Proverbs are the mirror in which a society looks at itself as well as the stage upon which it exposes itself to others. They describe its values, aspirations, and preoccupations, as well as the particular angle from which it sees and appreciates realities and behaviour; what we call a mentality or way of life is best pictured in them.

Fr Joseph Healey is a Maryknoll priest who has worked in East Africa for over 30 years and has extensive knowledge of indigenous oral tradition. There are a growing number of theologians who, like him, see this tradition as the African style *par excellence* of theologising. In fact, the phrase 'the fifth Gospel' is used to indicate those facets of Christian revelation already present in African religion. Oral literature and tradition have been called Africa's Old Testament, their 'unwritten Bible', in which there are striking similarities between African wisdom and Hebrew wisdom. It may be noted that the renowned biblical scholar St Jerome suggested (in the late 4th century AD) that those desirous of learning about the Christian faith through study of the Bible should begin by reading the wisdom literature of the Old Testament, before moving on to the gospels. There is also a venerable church tradition of using secular fables to illustrate homilies.

A number of parallels have been observed between African proverbs and Jesus' own sayings in the gospels, for example:

> God's rain falls even on the witch.
> What goes into the stomach is not lasting.
> You laugh at a person with a bad eye while you hide your own defects.

Fr Aylward Shorter has said:

> Proverbs and riddles are two closely related forms of didactic literature, in statement and question form. They play an important role in traditional African societies in the process by which the young are initiated to life.

Further, Pope John Paul II has himself commented, 'As vehicles of the wisdom and soul of the people, they are a precious source of material and of inspiration for the modern media.'

My opening illustrations suggest that, although with changing times some sayings will disappear, others will be adapted and new ones will take their place (so that in his lectures Professor Caird delighted to illustrate the process of semantic change within biblical literature). In the past decade considerable efforts have been made to baptise this oral culture into the service of evangelisation, not least in homiletics and catechetical instruction in East Africa where 'proverb catechesis' is now practised. So Fr Healey has sketched out a contextualised theology of mission, healing and the sacraments that incorporates a number of proverbial sayings:

> The patient person eats ripe fruit.

> Little by little the moon becomes full.
> Eyes that know how to wait put the crown on the head.

Here is a reminder of the waiting apostolate, surely a frequent experience for most Christians. Indeed, patience and perseverance are among the commonest words in the New Testament. Yet active proclamation of the Gospel is a daily demand, even if it takes time for the seeds of God's Word to take root and begin to grow. Hence the challenge implied in this riddle:

> As I walk along I spit out white shells.

White is a symbol of blessing, so the person who spits out sugar-cane pulp (and every Malawian loves sugarcane) – which may with some effort of the imagination be likened to 'white shells' –- is symbolically broadcasting God's good news. The call to evangelise means that fresh approaches are sometimes needed; Christians must be encouraged to adventure for Christ in new ways. And, as you will now expect, Africans have a phrase for it:

> The ant tries to eat the rock.

Despite those who mock the attempt and dismiss the Christian faith altogether, there may yet be surprises in store:

> A hidden, even contemptible, path is the one that leads to the highway.

After all, the Chewa people were once saved, not by the proud warriors of their tribe, but by a crazy man who recognised the enemy in their disguise:

> It was the mad person who saw the enemy approaching.

So too says St Paul: we are to be 'fools' for Christ's sake!
    Just published by our local Kachere Press is a marvellous collection of 2000 Chinyanja (or Chichewa) proverbs. It is edited by Fr Joseph Chakanza, a Catholic priest who teaches here at the university. I shall commend it to our own students as an important resource for evangelism.

Please pray for Christian preachers in Malawi, to be able to express their message in words that are understood and connect with people's lives.

OUT AND ABOUT
May 2001

ONE OF THE JOYS of training ordinands is to see them serving the Lord in later days, after ordination. Easter 2001 was such an opportunity: I was invited to celebrate and preach at St Martin's Church, Malindi, on the south-east shore of Lake Malawi. Just getting there proved an experience. Eventually there will be a proper road to the Mozambique border beyond it, but at present it is diabolical. It is not so much a matter of avoiding potholes as of choosing carefully those that are less than a foot deep.

We made it eventually at an average speed of 20 km an hour, to be greeted by the archdeacon and his new young deacon. There was time before the evening meal to be shown the immaculately maintained hospital. We were shocked to learn that at present there are only four nurses instead of the full complement of twenty or more. Half of the wards are therefore unable to accommodate patients, despite the urgent need to take in more. On a more positive note we heard about a number of new parish projects, together with good reports of our ex-student. 'He has good judgement', we were told, 'which he needs to exercise on a daily basis.' The following day the main Easter mass was of course packed, and I doubt if I've ever blessed so many babies in my life. Although we returned by the same route, the track seemed to have disintegrated even further!

The next weekend we made another long journey (but on tar roads), this time north to Mzuzu for the consecration of the new bishop of Northern Malawi viz. Chris Boyle, who hails from the diocese of Birmingham. This was a real gathering of the clans, with old friends appearing from Zambia and new ones from Malawi. It gave us a good opportunity to discuss the progress of various projects and to brief the bishops about our students. The Vice-President honoured the occasion, once again devoting most of his welcome speech to ways in which church and state could cooperate on AIDS initiatives. We followed local custom in presenting the college's gift to the new bishop with a song and a dance. Bishop Christopher will no doubt be down in Zomba once or twice a year for meetings of the college board.

This term particularly we have noticed the increasing impact of AIDS. Almost every day in chapel we are told of students granted leave of absence to attend funerals. Staff members are affected too, and their classes are then untaught for several days at a time. One day recently, only two of us were left in college, with three quarters of all the programmed lectures having to be cancelled. The same thing happens too with businesses and with government departments, resulting in weeks and months of delay everywhere. Letters and packets take up to three months now, after languishing in a mounting pile of unsorted mail.

Having mentioned in a recent report the advent of an Anglican colleague, I must now report his impending departure for further study in the United States. At the same time, though, a senior priest is coming back from the States to Zomba, where he will pursue doctoral study about the care of AIDS patients and their families in Malawi. He told us in a recent letter how un-Anglican he has found many of his experiences across the waters. Although American Episcopalians are generous in supporting African priests through higher degree courses in their own colleges, there is a suspicion that they also hope to infect some of the future African church leaders (from a more conservative background) with their well-known liberal thinking.

Our own research seminar is gathering momentum. One of my contributions has been a historical analysis of the Christian handling of loans/debt. I was quite surprised to discover the widespread misunderstanding by students of the biblical jubilee. The proposals in Leviticus 25 were designed to place a time limit on indebtedness, not to cancel any actual debt – it was Jesus himself who advocated the latter, as characteristic of God's own generous nature. The Jubilee campaign that climaxed in 2000 continues to need support so that further progress can be made in relieving Third World poverty. Yet it is not only Western countries that need to be reminded of the message: in Malawi it has been said that 30 per cent of the government's annual income is stolen. Since that figure is the one released by the government's own auditor, the actual amount is likely to be even more. Urgent steps must surely be taken here (as much as anywhere else in the world) to bridge the growing gap between rich and poor.

I am glad to say that, with some Anglican prompting, our programme of morning worship has become more flexible over the past few weeks. It is not easy in an ecumenical setting to make changes that will satisfy everyone, but for an experimental period we can now adapt more African ways of singing and use a wider range of liturgical material. As the one responsible for the lectionary I try to keep closer to the Christian calendar than happened previously (for example, for the first time we are very soon making provision for Ascension Day and Pentecost). We are also exploring ways of fostering spiritual growth, and of helping students to preach more effectively. At last, after nearly 25 years in existence, ZTC now has a proper syllabus for the course on sermon preparation.

A couple of donations from England have enabled all the Anglican ordinands to go on retreat in the past few weeks. Fr Stewart Lane, long experienced in working with young people, has been their conductor. At college we are so intent upon the academic courses that we have little enough time for reflection. There are personal challenges, of course, but also issues that require our collective attention. The Anglican Church in Malawi faces many significant changes, not so very different from those met also in England – for example, a shortage of clergy, and disaffection among young people who find things seemingly out of touch with their generation. As well as exchanging ideas with Fr Stewart, I've gained much also from Fr Rodney Hunter, a USPG missionary for many years here in Malawi. He spent several days staying with us before Easter.

The new college for Christian mission in the capital Lilongwe is currently under construction, and we have recently been to see the bishop to talk about its programmes. It will open its doors in January 2002 to equip men and women for various lay ministries, and especially for evangelism – within Malawi, or even in neighbouring countries such as Zambia where Chichewa is commonly spoken. At the moment I am assisting in the preparation of a syllabus for the college, trying to take into account its limited resources and the constraints on staffing. If this bears fruit, it will be a significant development for the grassroots life of the Anglican Church here. It certainly needs much support and prayer at this formative stage, especially as there is a divisive faction in the diocese of Lake Malawi which apparently hopes to turn the college into a 'born again' centre and even to train like-minded priests there.

Otherwise I have been trying to master the art of saying No. Strong pressure was put on me to take over as registrar for the theological board at the university, then as dean of studies at college. Both of these are administrative jobs, until now held by expatriates, each requiring a lot of time and patience (probably a recipe for a nervous breakdown). The registrar does not need to be an ordained person, as once again a lay person, preferably a Malawian, may be much better able to fill this role. Pressure to take on extra responsibilities is building from another direction too, but I recognise once again that I need to work within my limitations. My priority remains the task of teaching theology, with its attendant need for adequate preparation and reflection.

It is important too that I keep in touch with the Anglican Church both in Zomba and throughout Malawi, since it is here that our future priests will serve. Hence we welcome the occasional opportunities to visit parishes and outstations beyond our own, and invariably find much warmth and encouragement from priests and their congregations alike (exceptionally there is just one such colleague whose conversation returns rather too readily to his expanding list of desirable household goods!)

Please pray for those young in ministry, for bishop Christopher in Northern Malawi, and for those involved in planning the new Christian training college. Pray especially for the overcoming of any sectarian divisiveness among Malawian Anglicans.

A WEEK IN SARAH'S DIARY
June 2001

SUNDAY pm: Our visit to prison

Mothers Union and others have been raising money to buy soap, toothbrushes, sugar, tea and clothes for the prisoners. I joined an impressive parade of ladies who sang all the way from the church to the prison, where we divided into smaller groups to visit the 1000 or so prisoners. Our own group went to the women's unit. The women prisoners sang their thanks in response to our spontaneous hymns and prayers, and listened to our words of encouragement. It was very moving to be received so joyfully and gratefully.

MONDAY am: Village theft

Our daily visitor Duncan Mbale arrived very upset because his house (in reality no bigger than a garden shed) had been broken into, and his prize possessions taken: food, teapot, mug, hat, blanket. Thefts are on a rapid increase even in the villages, and old practices are changing. For example, people now dry their maize indoors instead of outdoors, even though this greater security does not allow the maize to be ventilated adequately in the process, and often results in the growth of a carcinogenic mould, which can be fatal if ingested.

TUESDAY am: Need of money

Saulo has been shivering with malaria, and had to be taken home with a dose of Fansidar. Nyasalandi's problem concerned the examination fees for his daughter: only one day is left before the cut-off point for entries. There has recently been a huge increase in all secondary school charges which most families cannot afford. We gave him what was required – but of course there are frequently other crises of this kind, such as expenses for a funeral or repairs to a damaged bike. Lloyd arrived later this morning, also asking for money. We were not sure about his need, knowing that he had recently turned down two gardening jobs. What he didn't tell us at the time (which we learnt later) was that he is dying of AIDS and has little strength. His wife is dying too, and there are two young children who need care.

WEDNESDAY am: The wives

On Wednesday mornings I meet regularly with some ordinands' wives, whom I help with English conversation and Bible readings for chapel worship. When I tested their geography recently by asking them to sketch a map showing places we had discussed, it was quite a revelation: England occupied a huge territory in their imagination, far bigger than the whole of Africa! Apart from our fascinating conversations, the wives are also prepared for hospital visiting, attend courses on AIDS, learn about home care and management, and of course explore aspects of the Christian faith. At the beginning of term sewing classes were delayed by a rat infestation, but have since proved to be a good opportunity to get to know the wives better. They are enthusiastic learners, and make little waistcoats with trousers or skirts for their toddlers. They had a sponsored praise recently in aid of a forthcoming retreat, combining in wonderful harmonies. Their children formed an excellent little choir too.

THURSDAY am: Hospital help

My morning is spent with children in the local children's ward. Most are from the villages, with little English. Some look very small and undernourished, so I am amazed when they tell me their actual age. Falasisiko at 14 years old is deaf and dumb, and was admitted with a broken leg: he looks only about 9. Shaibu has been in hospital for four months with his spine infected by TB, and so is very disabled. At first no treatment was available for him, but now with physiotherapy and medication he is much brighter and loves to do anything creative. But he still can't straighten his legs.

FRIDAY pm: Carolyn's plans

Our own orphan Carolyn has passed her recent exams! She has been unsure of her future, but now feels once again that she should take a nursing course. The best training is at St. Luke's, the mission hospital at Malosa. It is the first choice for treatment in our area – provided Malawians can raise the modest treatment fees – as standards are so much higher than at Zomba Central Hospital. Since the current nursing course is now underway, Carolyn has been looking elsewhere too. Another possible course has just been cancelled due to lack of government funding, although it may become viable later in the year (or so they hope).

SATURDAY am: Removal van!

Evason Mpulula's rent has just increased sharply, which he can't afford. A less expensive house in his wife's village is available, so I load up all their belongings in our truck. Most of the trip is on dirt roads, but we end in a pleasant location by a river. Local people come out to help carry the *katundu* to the mud and thatch house, where they now seem happily installed.

SUNDAY am: Village church

Rodney takes the service at St. Mary's, Chinamwali – a nearby outstation of St. George's Church, with a really thriving congregation. The people have nearly completed a new building around the site of the now demolished older and much smaller building (the vestry is still full of rubble). Most of the construction work was undertaken by members of the congregation, who also moulded and burnt their own bricks. A cheque from our last bishop in England enabled them to buy roofing materials. When the walls have been plastered and whitewashed, with extra benches installed inside, and the priest's house finished next door, it will become a separate parish. Most of the outstations are – as St Mary's has been until now – in the care of a catechist or lay 'chairman'. They seem to flourish and multiply without the detailed planning that would be necessary in the UK. So it was fittingly the lay leader who woke everyone up here this morning with dynamic alleluias to start them all singing and dancing.

Please pray for the local hospitals and their staff, and for God's blessing upon initiatives – like St Mary's – that bring faith and hope alive in the communities.

THE IMPACT OF AIDS
July 2001

EXACT STATISTICS for Malawi are hard to come by, but it is believed that out of a population of between 10 and II million people there are now at least 750,000 orphans under the age of 16. In Zomba district over 20,000 such orphans are registered, and in each sizeable village orphans are usually numbered in their scores rather than in single figures. A few orphanages exist in the main centres, but it is generally the extended families, or by default village communities, which care for these children.

At our theological college almost all married students have responsibility for other children apart from their own. Some of our ordinands may well be looking after two, three, four or more nephews and nieces. In fact, a rule has recently been introduced limiting the number of these orphans on campus to two per household. It often means that our ordinands' wives need to learn sewing or some other craft in order to make ends meet. When single students get married they will certainly not begin their marriages in childless fashion, as almost immediately they will be expected to take charge of parentless nephews and nieces. Staff members too report a steady increase in the number of their charges. For example, one lecturer has lost three sisters-in-law already this year (presumably to AIDS, but it is still generally shameful to admit the real cause of death); so from each of those households six or seven children are now in need of maternal care, a total of some twenty. There is thus enormous pressure on waged families to shoulder extra burdens. (We hear similar news from further south. In Lesotho in the mid 1980s AIDS was as yet unrecognised, but now some of our best students who went on to serve as priests in the parishes have already died.)

Households with a wage earner are nevertheless in a minority, and it is more often the older generation who end up caring for their grandchildren. Sarah has recently become involved with a care group at Songani. Although initially this focused on the needs of just a single village, it now covers a number of villages some miles to the east of Zomba. When it began in 1996 there were thus twenty orphans being looked after, but –

as other villages have joined in – several hundred more have since been registered. As the name Songani Community Care Group implies, it is the extended community that takes responsibility, so this is quite distinct from an orphanage and indeed has a much wider remit.

This was very much a local initiative, fostered by Kennedy Mpoya (an Adventist Christian) who, as a counsellor at St Luke's Hospital, Malosa, had become aware of the alarming number of deaths in his village. He realised that, with the hospital having for reasons of limited space to send a number of AIDS patients home, many of these were then unable to cope either with their own needs or with any children in their family. So he rallied the local people to pool whatever resources they could spare and offered to coordinate their responses to the growing crisis. They are now grouped into four districts, each with about 18 or 20 volunteers. They make a small personal donation of 7 kwacha each week, as well as looking after the youngest children in two nursery centres and growing maize on a couple of plots of land to help feed those in greatest need. *NB Malawi lies south of the equator, so planting takes place around October at the start of the rainy season, with harvesting in April when the dry season begins.*

Altogether there are well over two hundred households which take care of the roughly 350 orphans. Although the guardians usually look after just one or two of these children, there are those with as many as four or five. It is also clear that, while some of the guardians may be younger women, many are elderly grandmothers with little enough to feed extra mouths and clothe extra bodies – including maybe sick or dying adults. At Songani every effort is made to keep the primary-age children at school (which at this level is free in Malawi, except for the cost of a school uniform), and to raise money to pay for the older ones to attend secondary school. Once or twice a month all the orphans receive a bar of soap, and those not yet at school are given a meal each day of *Likuni phala* (a mixture of soya, flour, maize, with some sugar).

Several local village craftsmen are also engaged regularly to teach life skills such as carpentry, welding and brick laying, with the girls learning how to sew and to make (or alter) clothes. Without parents of their own, the traditional learning acquired in daily family life needs to be specifically imparted in other ways. None the less, older children have to assume many extra responsibilities – caring for their siblings and fulfilling basic needs by fetching water, hoeing the 'garden', and performing so-called menial tasks. Even while one of their parents is growing weaker with what is popularly known as 'slim' disease, they may already have shouldered a disproportionate share of the burden of care. AIDS is still feared, and there are many myths about how it is passed on – for example, through merely touching someone already infected, or their clothing.

Orphans living in or near Songani are clearly very fortunate to have a far-sighted person like Mr Mpoya in their midst. He is meticulous in checking and recording all the details of (e.g.) finance and attendance, and brings professional training to bear upon the project. Elsewhere, such skills and commitment are often less readily available, as is evidenced by the number of children begging on the streets of the main towns and cities. Efforts by non-governmental organisations to provide for them and to give them schooling have generally been unsuccessful, as the rewards of begging have a more immediate appeal. But those who are beggars today will be criminals and drug pushers tomorrow, and the fabric of Malawian society will then be tested even further.

In all of this, it needs to be remembered that the root cause of HIV/AIDS infection is not necessarily seen in medical terms in an often pre-scientific culture. It is by no means obvious why (for example) an imprudent sexual encounter or the use of a contaminated needle several years in the past can lack any apparent consequences for quite a long time. It is more natural to link causes and effects much more closely together. Hence, in a village where several deaths occur within a short space of time due to AIDS, there can often be witchcraft accusations, with a great deal of fear, hostility and malevolence towards already unpopular neighbours. Sadly too, the message often preached from the pulpit is not one of compassion, but a proclamation of God's wrath, one who is punishing the wicked for their sins. Here is an issue which we regularly explore with students (and their wives) within college – the fundamental question, 'What is the Gospel which as Christians we need to share?'

Please pray for Kennedy, his team of helpers and guardians at Songani, and the sick, bereaved and orphaned in their care.

THE RESPONSE TO AIDS
August 2001

IN THE MIDDLE OF ZOMBA is a government-funded poster of a young woman brushing off a young man, apparently on heat, with the words 'No condom, no way'. The irony is that this poster is next to the entrance of the main Presbyterian Church in town, and all the churches of Malawi are solidly opposed to the condom culture, believing that it encourages people to be too easily promiscuous. The government message appears to say nothing more than 'Go ahead – so long as you take precautions against infection'. Of course, the churches want to halt the spread of AIDS, but they do not believe that the prevalent culture of casual liaisons should be so readily condoned. Unfortunately not all our visitors and partners from overseas (Anglicans included) respect the churches' position here. Some have even campaigned blatantly against it, thus undermining the work being done. It is not simply a matter of providing condoms (a proportion of which are dumped on Third World countries because they fail to meet quality control tests elsewhere). Important issues about personal relationships, moral responsibility and indeed attitudes of male chauvinism have certainly to be addressed as well.

What are the official facts and figures of HIV infection in Malawi? With a current prevalence admitted to be at least 16%, it is estimated that 20-25% of men and women currently employed in the urban-based sector (where the prevalence rate is much higher) will die by the year 2005. The number of those being orphaned is currently 70,000 per annum but is likely to triple over the next ten years. A recent health survey estimates that in extra-marital or casual liaisons condom use is around 30%. A growing attitude among the young, in knowledge of rapidly declining life-expectancy (now reduced to about 37 years) seems much inclined to disregard all warnings. In other words, posters do little to alter the fatalism expressed in the words of Isaiah, 'Let us eat and drink (and be merry with sex), for tomorrow we die.'

Every sector of life is affected here. All the public utilities suffer staffing casualties and absences, reducing whatever pretence at efficiency they may once have boasted. Men and women working for private employers begin to lose their stamina, and have to give up a precious job, thus abandoning their one source of income. Every family known to us (which in Africa is understood as an extended family) has a number of orphans in their care. There may be perhaps 200 orphans in a small village or 600-700 in a large one, which makes it less and less easy for the family network to cope. Orphanages are springing up. Some of these are well-managed and attempt to provide sound training in life skills, but others may be readier to exploit the situation by using any local or overseas funding for personal gain. Whichever way, feeding extra mouths is never easy.

Every day for the past week in chapel our Principal has announced the absence of students or staff who have gone to attend a funeral. It has seriously affected the teaching programme to a degree not noticed in the previous year. And of course AIDS hits the churches and their leaders seemingly as much as it hits non-churchgoers. Priests and ministers have died, as have their wives, although people will usually speak of TB or malaria as the killer. A colleague looking recently through old college photographs was stunned to realise that possibly a quarter of those in training in the mid-1980s are now dead. Although HIV testing is carried out before students reach us, we cannot assume that the college has a complete bill of health. One of the pressures upon us has been the rapid expansion of our numbers, without an equivalent expansion of married quarters. Men here without their wives for one or even two years are exposed to temptation. Pray for them, indeed pray for us all here, to remain faithful to our calling.

In Dr Banda's time AIDS did not officially exist. There were notices at the airports asking visitors not to bring it into the country. But then, under his regime, droughts and crop failure never happened either, and anyone voicing criticism was liable to be liquidated. Public acknowledgement of the situation was much slower in coming than, say, in Uganda, which has made significant reductions in its rate of infection. There is now, I believe, a Ugandan government directive requiring priests and ministers who conduct a funeral to make plain to the congregation if AIDS was the principal cause of death. In Malawi it is only now that care schemes for AIDS sufferers are getting off the ground, along with massive attempts at public education. At a major conference in February 2001 the churches and the government agreed to cooperate much more fully, despite their different emphases. So other posters are beginning to emerge bearing the starker message, 'Malawians – change your behaviour!'

Let me mention one remarkable initiative that is bearing much fruit here and is even finding an export market in other parts of Africa. The *Why Wait?* programme has been growing for several years under the inspired guidance of two American missionaries in Zomba. They came here to teach in the university, well qualified in areas of child development and counselling after many years' experience as lecturers in the States. They now report that their university classes are bursting at the seams, with a majority of men in attendance – although I should qualify that comment by adding that both universities and nursing schools are 'temporarily suspended' as a result of government mishandling of their funds, with money for tertiary education having been diverted into ministerial expense accounts. Hopefully the *Why Wait?* training will resume soon. It provides a broad coverage of family and personal relationships within a Christian framework. Its greatest impact has been in secondary schools up and down the country, many of which have now adopted its three-year syllabus. In one such school, in the year before its introduction, there were over 80 unwanted teenage pregnancies: because of the Christian commitment of the head teacher to the new programme and the dedication of his teachers, within two years that figure has been reduced to just one new pregnancy.

The Gospel that we preach and try to live in company with Christians from many other churches is not a tired, out-of-date message. There is no call to revise our moral teaching in line with modern thinking. It expresses the love that lies at the heart of God's initiative to enable our human fruition as bearers of his image.

Please pray for those infected with HIV/AIDS, and for the readiness not only to care for them but to help others who may be led astray by false desires and teachings.

NEW DEVELOPMENTS
September 2001

THE DRY SEASON started early this year, unlike 2000, and scarcely a drop fell from April onwards. But at least in Zomba the Mulunguzi dam remains full, and by the end of July the water board appeared to have finished repairing the infrastructure of pipes and purification plants. So, after 18 months of collecting water in buckets and cans, we can now turn the taps on and get a reliable flow. The electricity supply is still interrupted, but in most cases this is because someone has brought down an overhead cable in the process of felling a tree.

At least in the dry season we can make visits to the otherwise inaccessible outstations. For the first time, we looped around the far side of Zomba mountain, and visited Fr Onaika at Chingali parish. As in a number of places a new and enlarged church is being built, and the settled warm weather enables the congregation to mould and fire their own hand-made bricks. I've recently been transporting bags of cement to two newly-built churches on the edge of Zomba, which is continually expanding. When I subsequently celebrated and preached at one of these churches (Likhubula), I came away with a well-trussed live hen by way of thanks!

Last Sunday I was once again at St. Mary's, Chinamwali within the growing township on the eastern side of Zomba, just over a mile away from where we live. It is actually nearer to us than St George's. It was most encouraging to see that their newly enlarged church is now virtually completed. Since our last visit the sanctuary and vestry have been finished, the walls plastered and painted, and the floor coloured and sealed. The singing here is magnificent, with a couple of superb drummers accompanying the choir. Altogether it felt as if we were worshipping in a vast cathedral.

The college campus is also expanding its capacity, with new family units. I've been glad to have been involved in advising on the revision of selection procedures for new students. There is no shortage of candidates, but what is essential is to find the ones with real commitment. There are two main problems arising within Malawi that would scarcely occur within the UK. First, parish priests here find it hard to write anything critical about someone who has been put forward, so their weaknesses can sometimes surface too late. And secondly, even potentially strong candidates may be more interested in acquiring a diploma or degree than in following a priestly vocation. The truth is that a few see Zomba Theological College as a free route to further education, provided by the churches. Similar attitudes occur, so I am told, among those seeking admission to the Catholic seminaries. Entry to universities (of which there are now two) is more demanding, both in terms of entry standards and fees. Some of those who complete their studies do not stay long in the service of the church, but perhaps enter teaching or the civil service for more highly paid jobs.

As we come towards the end of our second academic year here, we look forward to the graduation ceremonies, at which the guest of honour is to be an Anglican, the distinguished Vice-Chancellor David Rubadiri. He and his wife are among our congregation at St George's, although in Dr Banda's time they were among those forced into exile. We hope and pray that those who leave us for ordination in the next month or two will fulfil all our expectations.

The churches in Malawi do of course encourage suitably gifted clergy to take their studies further. Such men, it is hoped, will be the leaders in tomorrow's church as well as the lecturers at ZTC. Of my colleagues, three have just begun higher degrees in the USA, Canada and Britain. This inevitably puts those of us left behind under some strain. As I write, it is not clear whether these academic colleagues will be replaced, but I suspect that in January 2002 I shall find myself with a heavier teaching load, as well as extra pastoral responsibilities within the college. I have therefore declined (for the time being) to accept the further role of acting priest-in-charge of St. George's.

In fact, there are some very gifted lay people in the congregation, and with suitable priestly assistance they should be able to steer the church through the next ten months until the rector (who is on study leave in the UK) returns. Soon after that, it is expected that the diocese of Southern Malawi will divide into two. St. Paul's, Blantyre (where Charles Mackenzie's bones are now interred) will remain as the cathedral for the diocese of

Southern Malawi, while St. George's, Zomba is likely to become the cathedral for the northerly division.

We have been very grateful to receive some tangible gifts from supporters overseas. A chalice, paten and ciborium have been passed on to one of our outstanding young priests; 200 redundant Anglican service books – almost in mint condition, with markers and protective covers – have enabled every priest and ordinand to receive a copy, which will certainly provide them with extra liturgical resources; new shelves have been added in the college library to house a number of donated books, although good books on ethics and spirituality are still badly needed; some redundant typewriters have found a home in the wives' school.

Recently I have undertaken further research into how much theological material can be easily found and downloaded off the internet. I was pleased to have discovered an increasing number of websites with primary sources (e.g. the early church fathers) in English translation – even though there are inevitably too many useless or junk sites that could mislead the unwary. This has enabled me to put together a book entitled *Jubilee Reflections: Rich and Poor in Christian Perspective*, which will soon be published here by Kachere Press, an arm of the university department of Theology and Religious Studies. It will be printed by the Montfort Fathers at their press in Balaka. This was formerly known as Freedom Printing Press, because of its key role in copying the historic letter of the Catholic bishops for distribution in Lent 1992, which sparked off Kamuzu Banda's downfall – yet not before his Young Pioneers had retaliated by attacking the premises. The book should be available both in USA and in UK (here through the African Book Collective in Oxford). My hope is that students here will also be encouraged to explore digital resources when up-to-date books are not available in the library. Computers are beginning to be a little more familiar in Malawi, although the real headache will be their maintenance, especially with multiple users.

Please pray for the people of St George's, Zomba, and for the diocese of Southern Malawi as it prepares for future changes.

ORPHAN SUPPORT
October 2001

CAROLYN has this year been attending a series of computer courses at the university, and now a further one to improve her typing skills. She takes her exam after Christmas. The university has now remained closed for many months, as have the main nursing schools, through lack of government funding. It has not been an easy year for her: she visited her younger sister day after day, and saw her gradually waste away with AIDS. Last year this same sister's baby died, and before that her other sister, as did both her parents some years ago. The periods before and after each funeral are inevitably very sad indeed.

Sarah continues to visit the children's ward in Zomba General Hospital regularly, taking art and craft materials for the children to use. The children look forward to this so much, as there is little else for them to do.

Orphan care has also taken up much more of her time, with regular visits to Songani. To recap: Songani Community Care helps to support, feed, educate and train hundreds of AIDS orphans in several villages to the east of Zomba, who remain in the care of their extended families, perhaps a grandmother, or maybe just an older sibling. Support is also offered to those living with HIV/AIDS. This self-help project began five years ago on the initiative of the local people, with the hope that it would become self-supporting. With inflation in Malawi running at approximately 30 per cent, the project was fortunate to receive a grant from War on Want for each of two years. This year very heavy rains and flooding in the wet season resulted in exceptionally low maize yields, resulting in escalating prices in local and imported products – and a looming time of hardship, the so-called 'hunger months' (from now through to March) when food supplies will remain at rock bottom. Relief should come in early April when the new harvest is expected. Until then, many people will of necessity have at most one meal a day, which for some may mean (e.g.) roots, grasses or snakes.

Already the monthly cost of maize for the orphans has risen steeply: in April a 50kg sack could be bought for 250 kwacha, whereas six months later the price is 850 kwacha. This means that somewhere in the region of £600 sterling (£1.50 per child) is needed for the feeding budget each month, without including those necessary extras such as soap. Although we received an official letter from the depot in Blantyre allowing a regular load of 30 sacks to be collected there for the orphans, this supply – which came from Tanzania – has now run out, which means that Mr Mpoya will have to search further afield in the coming months.

The village helpers work very hard themselves, meeting each week to discuss problems, running their own garden, performing drama to explain about AIDS, and getting in skilled workers to teach the children useful crafts such as carpentry or metalwork.

You may like to use this prayer (written by Sarah for Songani):

> Dear Lord, we put the whole Songani care group into your hands; for you already know the hearts and minds of everyone here, and you know where the greatest needs lie. We ask you to bless all those living in fear of disease, those who are sick and suffering because of the AIDS virus, those who are dying and who worry about the children they are leaving behind, and those who undertake to care for these children. We pray that as a community we can come together in your name, and that you will show us a way to see how best to be effective in our care and support of those devastated by this disease. We pray that your loving hand will be with us even in the difficult times that lie ahead. Uphold us in our commitment to each other; strengthen and deepen our faith in your power to save and to heal. Amen.

On a happier note it was wonderful to have my brother Malcolm and his wife Elizabeth for a visit lasting just over two weeks in August, a very pleasant month for weather. A new departure was to rent a bungalow on one of the tea estates not far from the Mulanje range for one weekend. Its unexpected feature was hot water provided through the cold tap! We hope to see others from our family around Christmas.

Just before our visitors came there was another 'first' – officiating at a Malawian wedding, at St. Paul's Cathedral in Blantyre. James, a chemical engineer from Staffordshire (and a former chemical weapons inspector in Iraq, where – so he tells us - nothing noteworthy was ever detected) who worships at St. George's, married a Malawian girl called Prisca. So there were plenty of Malawian customs to be observed, such as the spectacle of bridesmaids preceding the bride into the church, dancing up the aisle. Immediately in front of the bride came the flower girl strewing petals, with a page-boy carrying a prayer book. At the reception we participated fully in *perekani perekani*, whose simplest translation is 'give, give'. Under different headings, the guests leave their places and dance forwards (and back again) with cash gifts for bride and groom. Each person is called to their feet several times, as they qualify under headings such as 'those who are related to the groom', 'those who work with the bride', 'those who live in the bride's village'. These cash gifts are in lieu of bringing a wedding present in kind. Here, and we understand at most other Malawian weddings, the liquid refreshment was non-alcoholic – the ubiquitous Fanta and Coca-Cola being particularly popular. By contrast, at village festivals it is likely that home-made beer will be brewed in considerable quantities, and consumed to the very last drop!

The mail in Malawi remains as slow and unreliable as ever, so this is probably the best opportunity to bid all our friends a happy Christmas, and to thank you once again for your support and your prayers.

Please pray for honesty and justice in the sharing of meagre food supplies as the months of hardship begin.

In the Mulanje mountains

THE NEED FOR REPARATION
November 2001

LAST YEAR there was a special focus upon Jubilee 2000, the campaign founded in 1993 to promote Third World debt relief. When Third World countries themselves joined the campaign in 1998, they pressed for debt cancellation, but this has now been enlarged to considerations of *reparation*. It is an important issue, although it must not be thought to exonerate Third World countries themselves from some responsibility for their own indebtedness. Certainly much of Malawi's debt can be traced back over twenty or thirty years to Dr Banda's creation of Lilongwe as his new centre of government and to his building of extra palaces for himself, when his borrowing coincided with a huge escalation of world oil prices and a period of rapid inflation.

Yet the issue of reparation will not go away, nor is it necessarily solely one for Western governments to consider. Although the churches are in the forefront of campaigning on behalf of the world's poor and are agents of much well-targeted aid, there is need to examine their own mission history very carefully. Did (no doubt well-intentioned) missionaries contribute to the dispossession of tribal lands, either by appropriating some to their own use or by giving tacit support to settlers who did the same? How far in bringing the Christian faith did they – at times unnecessarily or through ignorance – disrupt the culture that they found?

Further questions then arise. Is it possible to assess where the line runs between exploitation and development? Can we distance ourselves from the actions of our forebears, if in some degree we are the beneficiaries or at least are perceived to be their moral and spiritual heirs? Although the West (along with the churches) has been fairly generous with aid in recent decades, it is legitimate to ask how such funds compare with the profits generated through mining and farming both in imperial days and into the present, and whether there is not still a balance to be corrected. The question is, Who is in debt to whom?

In Malawi white-owned farms and estates were never very extensive in comparison with Zimbabwe and South Africa, nor did the number of colonisers and other newcomers together ever extend beyond about 10,000. In fact, titles to land were scrutinized fairly rigorously by the early governors, and it was later under Dr Banda that much common land was seized for the use of his African cronies. Even land and property belonging to the Anglican Church of Malawi was taken, and not all of it has yet been handed back. So if there is to be a squaring of accounts, it must certainly not be done with any racial or religious bias. If this could be eliminated in Zimbabwe too, whose rapid disintegration is now destabilizing Malawi's own investment prospects, there is the potential through regional cooperation to put bitterness behind and to take advantage of trade and tariff barriers that are little by little being eroded in Africa's favour. Even if globalization has its ruthless downside, there is a growing global awareness that we belong together for good and ill. If one suffers, all suffer – and therefore that it is no longer in anyone's real interest for the indignities of the past to be perpetuated today.

For John Paul II, the dawn of this third millennium has seemed a golden opportunity to try to come to terms with the past. He has pushed forward with hopes for ecumenical rapprochement, not least with the Orthodox Churches. At the same time he has seen the need for healing gestures in paving the way for reconciliation on other fronts. How remarkable that he has confessed some of the Church's past mistakes in meetings with Jewish and Muslim leaders. Peace and unity in the world, he has so vividly demonstrated, cannot proceed without a degree of humility and an awareness of one's own errors. He has effectively adopted the words of Nehemiah, at a time of post-exilic reconstruction, 'I and my father's house have sinned' (Neh 1.6). Such admissions are now recognised as a necessary part of 'just peace-making' – a phrase that is beginning to be used in parallel with (or perhaps even to replace) the centuries-old term 'just war'.

In other parts of the world it is good to note that certain Christian Churches have given similar prominence to this vital task of acknowledging past failings and shortcomings. Thus, in 1993 an apology was issued in the name of Canadian Christians for the imposition of an alien schooling system which did nothing to respect, let alone to foster, the native Indian culture. The following year Anglicans in Japan (where their church is known as

Nippon Sei Ko Kai) put out *A Statement of War Responsibility*, admitting guilt for not preventing or challenging atrocities that took place. Our present day 'blame culture' would like to force all sorts of other confessions, no doubt in the hope of converting these into hard cash. But that is to miss the point. The Pope suggests that we should have a moratorium on blaming others, and instead should explore our own collective or individual consciences.

To do this is not a sign of weakness, a betrayal of what 'our' cause has traditionally stood for; nor is it a white flag of surrender in the teeth of hostile pressure. In reality it betokens the maturity to recognize that truth has sometimes been distorted and facts have been concealed, that wrongs have been perpetrated (if not wilfully, at least through arrogance or insensitivity) by our forebears and maybe even by ourselves, and that none of us has an adequate defence when arraigned in God's court of reckoning. We may well act, and saints and heroes of earlier days will certainly have so acted too, in good faith and with sincere Christian intent; and yet all of us may on reflection have cause for regret. Whether in thought, word or deed, our good intentions will not have rendered us inerrant or infallible. Nor is it only for past actions that we need to admit responsibility. In the inextricable global linkages of the present, we are beginning to understand ever more clearly how environmental uses, industrial expansion, international trade (etc) impact in different ways upon every country of the world – including those not apparently party to particular developments.

Contrition before God allows him to work through us anew in refashioning his world. It looks to him to forgive and to heal the divisions and injustices we have brought about ourselves, perhaps heedlessly, because of our limited perceptions. It displays faith in God's power to overcome the dead weight of the past and the impasses of the present. Perhaps penitence on our part can be a vital witness to others in attracting their faith, encouraging them to place their hopes alongside ours? Is there in fact any better starting point to address the tensions, suspicions and longstanding feuds, whether in secular situations such as the land and compensation issues of Southern Africa, or in religious contexts where too readily we have come to accept animosity and polarization as the Christian norm?

God has surely endowed all of us with many blessings to be used for the common good. One day we shall be called to account for our stewardship: will we have spent our energies in humbly pursuing that good; or will we, as some Africans may still find themselves, be consumed with regrets, ever-ready to complain how our birthright has been taken away?

In the Bible there are several stories of rivalry within families, not all of which end in bitterness and recrimination. In the Genesis saga of Jacob, who cheats his brother Esau out of his inheritance, may be seen a paradigm of many injustices perpetrated over land and resources in Africa. Yet in the end the brothers are reconciled, and in complementary ways they both gain in spiritual stature: Jacob through his contrition, and Esau through his magnanimity, so that conflict and blame become alike redundant.

Please pray for the readiness to accept one's own failings and to be generous in forgiveness towards those who have wronged us.

THE ETHICAL DIMENSION OF COMMUNITY
December 2001

The peace of the Lord be with you!

BENEZET BUJO is a distinguished Catholic priest who has worked for many years, both in Africa and in Europe, as a moral theologian. Some of his writings have been published by Paulines Publications in Nairobi, run by the Daughters of St Paul. In the spirit of Vatican II they encourage the work of inculturating the Gospel message using all available means of communication, and could well be regarded as the leading religious publishers in Africa.

One of Bujo's most important books is *The Ethical Dimension of Community* (in German, 1993, but in English translation 1998). He lays great emphasis upon the traditional role played by the community in reaching decisions. For example, in Malawi a marriage is not just the romantic dream of two individuals who fall in love. Their two families have to be properly consulted, a process in which the man or woman is represented by a go-between, usually the maternal uncle on each side. The engagement ceremony involves all the family members of the man being introduced to those of the woman, and vice versa. Each family then undertakes to support the couple, and if things should go wrong in the future, the go-betweens have to meet, to confer with each other over what steps may need to be taken. A marriage can certainly not be terminated without family consent. 'The individual,' Bujo writes, 'needs the support of the whole extended family; marital harmony, children's education and economic life, all this can be successful only if carried out together.'

The danger, not so clearly seen by Bujo, is that family or clan interests may at times prevail to the detriment of the individual's well-being. Luciano Nervi, a Montfort Father, has commented:

> [The African] is not encouraged to think as an individual but rather as a member of the extended family ... conformity to the group is the supreme value.

Nevertheless, the African perspective is an important corrective to the prevailing individualism of the West. It has led to some criticism of the 1948 UN Declaration of Universal Human Rights, which of course pre-dated the independence of most African countries. The hesitation is that it lays too much emphasis upon personal rights rather than on corporate responsibilities. Thus, what holds for family life is (in theory at least) applicable to the wider sphere. It was still true when we lived in Lesotho in the 1980s that, if there was an important public issue needing to be faced, the chief would call a *pitso*, a village gathering that would meet to discuss, until consensus on the matter was reached. There was no pre-imposed time limit: talking might go on until the cows came home, not just that same day, but if necessary the next day, and the day after that as well. If the issue was a wider one, affecting other villages, the local chief would then go on to confer with his counterparts elsewhere until, once again, consensus was reached. Everyone present had the right to speak and to be heard, but especially the elders, whose experience and whose knowledge of tradition was highly respected. These spoke not only for themselves but also for the ancestors, the true guardians of the community. It should be noted too, that Western rules of debate are a continent apart. Thus when a senior African bishop was ruled out of order at the 1998 Lambeth Conference it was felt by other African bishops to be shockingly disrespectful.

Most other African societies have, or in the past have had, their own equivalents of the *pitso*. Bujo refers to them generally as 'palavers'. It will be clear already that there is plenty of room for misunderstanding and friction when European models of decision-making start to replace the palaver. A palaver is clearly an organ of democracy, but of a very different kind from the winner-takes-all style of majority voting preferred in the West. The Westminster model of rival political parties is a sure recipe for conflict in Africa. Its introduction can indeed be seen sometimes as a backward step, making for a new tribalism. This was the situation in Lesotho, where different Christian churches aligned themselves with the various political parties. It seems to obtain here in Malawi today. It is, for example, quite beside the point to ask what policies a campaigning party would wish to implement (I once naively asked such a question, and was met with a completely bemused look). Obviously the winner of an election shares the victory spoils, such as access to overseas aid, with his own tribe – his supporters. African politics is therefore largely about patronage, not policy. A constituency which has voted for an opposition MP can scarcely expect to be rewarded as well as a loyal constituency with, for example, better roads, bridges, clinics or schools.

How far this is the legacy of a hasty transfer of colonial power and how far it is the continuing pressure from major donors to see their version of democracy in place, is open to debate. Bujo, however, believes that the African instinct is for communitarianism, which is not 'a dual where defeat of one of two adversaries is aimed at ... (but) a form of mutual assistance.' It is 'a process of talking and listening', a dialogue searching for the common good. He insists that it is more than rational discourse, for 'without communal relationship one can neither find his or her identity nor learn to think.'

Descartes would have to modify his thinking in Africa and say, *Cognatus sum ergo sum* ('I am known, therefore I am' – I exist only in relation to others) for which there are many African proverbial equivalents, such as the famous Zulu saying, *Umuntu ngumuntu nagabantu* ('a person is a person because of other people'). There is an obvious resonance here with the Christian understanding of God himself as Trinitarian. In particular, it was Gregory of Nazianus in the late 4th century who suggested that the 'persons' of the Trinity are named after their mutual relationships, each one more expressive of a divine interaction than of an individual characteristic.

It will be evident by now that the traditions of palaver in Africa are more in keeping with the spirit of Christ than many of the procedures found today even in the Christian Church. In the present soul-searching of the Anglican Communion, which is in danger of falling apart, it needs to be pointed out that the fraternal spirit of the Lambeth Fathers from 1867 onwards was always consultation rather than legislation, a tradition very different in spirit from the factional strife that can divide synods (and is threatening to do so here in Malawi as well). Some have perhaps forgotten that the Greek original of 'synod' means literally 'together on the way'. So a reminder may be necessary that simply to achieve a voting majority can be far from discerning the truth in love, and that to work to a scheduled timetable is not quite the same as allowing the spirit to 'blow where he wills'. Indeed, one may ask, how much conflict in the Church is born of impatience and intolerance? How far is there little more than a desire to impose one's own stance on others, and as quickly as possible?

There may of course often be frustrations with the slow pace at which life proceeds and with which changes are made, but is that not to be preferred to a ruthless hastiness which leaves a trail of wreckage behind it? Did Christ himself preach that 'might is right', or that truth can be determined by a show of hands? Even the argumentative St. Paul has room for the slower thinkers: `Sinning against your brethren and wounding their conscience when it is weak, you sin against Christ' (1 Cor 8.12).

Jesus was undoubtedly a 'three mile an hour' God. He walked at a human pace, he spoke in earthy symbols, he resisted the devil's triumphalism, and rejected the royal road to success. He died as a minority of one, not even sure whether his closest friends had grasped the point. I think myself he might be found anonymously in barefooted rags here in Africa, as once he took refuge in a stable. The question is, would anyone give him admittance to their parliamentary or synodical debates?

Please pray for the readiness in all debate to listen to others, striving to reach mutual understanding and agreement.

YEAR 2002

Pied Kingfisher
In plentiful numbers, hence easily seen, along the Shire river - also the habitat for giant, pygmy and malachite kingfishers.

Drying maize cobs
These enormous woven baskets (*nkhokwe*) allow air to circulate
around the harvested cobs, thus inhibiting mould in the drying process.
After a poor harvest the baskets may be half empty,
inadequate to feed a family for the year ahead.

WITCHCRAFT BELIEFS
January 2002

WHEN PLANNING to spend Christmas 2001 with family in England, the question of house security in Zomba had to be considered. Burglaries are fairly common in Malawi and are not confined to homes that belong to the relatively affluent minority. Our own bishop was burgled recently, and the Roman Catholic bishop of Zomba suffered two attacks in close succession – but so did the poorest of the poor in our nearest local village. Thus Duncan, our recycling agent (who calls each morning for his breakfast, collects our waste papers and packaging, and usually brings us a cabbage or a paw-paw in exchange), had his plastic raincoat and other meagre possessions taken from the small shed where he lives. We have a wire fence installed by my predecessor and employ a watchman, but I suspect African protective measures might be even more effective. If, before going on leave, I had summoned a *singanga* ('medicine man') and he had buried charms around the property with suitably impressive incantations, word would rapidly have spread that thieves intruded at their own risk, and could well expect misfortune, sickness or even death to follow swiftly. In the event, I felt a liaison with magical forces might not have been quite what is expected of a Christian missionary!

Witchcraft beliefs are not of course restricted to Africans. Many parts of the world have experienced them, both in the past, as in biblical times (Isa 19.3) and in medieval Europe, and in the present – including contemporary England. It was the usual policy of British colonial administration to prohibit the practice of witchcraft in its territories, and to ignore those who brought forward accusations. It regarded these beliefs as primitive, baseless and repugnant, needing to be repressed by law and eliminated through the spread of enlightened civilisation. Seldom, however, was policing adequate to achieve these aims. In actual practice, when administrative powers were delegated to traditional authorities (the chiefs), they reverted to 'native law and custom'. In Malawi, perhaps to prevent public lynching, Dr Banda's government allowed for the trial and conviction of witches. Yet very recently official notice of sorcery has been taken too in an Anglican diocese back in England. 1998 saw the introduction in Somerset of a rite to counteract it which includes these words, 'Cleanse us and our generation from any adverse effect of the past.' Around the same time a young woman in my English parish told me that in hospital she had seen the adjacent patient apparently praying at her bedside and had remarked to her, 'how refreshing to find a fellow Christian.' She was dumbfounded by the response, 'No, I belong to a coven, and I'm praying for the death of all the new-born babies here.' I am now less confident than I once was (as a student of mathematical sciences) that such malignancy is wholly ineffective.

The marked increase in witchcraft accusations in sixteenth- and early seventeenth-century Britain has been attributed by Keith Thomas to two principal, but related, factors: one is the Reformation itself, and the other is the rise of Protestant individualism. He argues that when misfortune struck and uncanny things happened in earlier times, the Catholic Church had its own armoury of protection. Relics, pilgrimages, the prayers of the saints were allied with the power of exorcism. When these were written off in the name of scriptural religion (conveniently overlooking the many and varied ways our Lord confronted evil), the ordinary Christian was left feeling vulnerable. At the same time his social world was being challenged and changed, and growing prosperity left many feeling guilty about those in their community who were being left behind. Thus, it was typically the poor neighbour turned away at the door whose subsequent curse was most feared. In time the Poor Laws and eventually the Welfare State quietened people's consciences by providing alternative relief.

In a fascinating new book *Witchcraft, Power and Politics*, the ethnographer Isak Niehaus has charted the more recent history of witchcraft accusations in the Northern Transvaal. He sees such beliefs as a form of protest by the weak for their self-protection – as it were, a popular mode of political action. He suggests witch-hunting can be seen as 'a creative attempt to eliminate evil', and indirectly a warning to the rich and powerful to redistribute their wealth:

> Villagers situationally invoke witchcraft beliefs as they encounter perplexing events, experience prolonged conflict in marriage, or suffer unspeakable

> misfortune ... [they have] less to do with civilization and African identity than with their experiences of misery, marginalization, illness, poverty and insecurity.

And perhaps their instinct is right. Their life-situation is indeed the result of human processes, of choices made by others which exclude them from the good things that life can offer. To say that an illness is the result of viral infection or that poverty is the fruit of impersonal market forces is to temporise. In the end one cannot deny that human actions and decisions have been involved somewhere along the line. If there has been any mistake by those who feel victimised, it is perhaps to seize too readily upon someone conveniently at hand who can be blamed.

Niehaus examines briefly the response of Churches in South Africa to this phenomenon. He notes that 'only the ministers of mission (mainline) Churches discouraged the belief in witches.' Thus, a Methodist remarked, 'If people are sick, they're sick, if people are dead, they're dead. We must not ask why.' But Niehaus points out that such teachings had, and have, little impact compared with the hugely popular Zionist churches which actively recognize (like medieval Catholicism) the existence of witchcraft beliefs, and practise appropriate remedies. This of course can also be seen as our Lord's answer to suffering in his own day. A later scientific or supposedly rational culture may not give credence to the existence of personal devils nor of individual evil spirits, but Jesus' ministry was effective because it was appropriately inculturated within 1st century Judaism.

Nevertheless his response to evil was also exercised on a more cosmic scale, as St. Paul recognized. There is evil operative within this world, whether or not it can be ascribed to 'principalities and powers', to other demonic sources, or simply to human malevolence: our faith is that in Christ and the power of his Holy Spirit it has met its match.

I do not conclude, though, that I can dispense with my watchman and rely wholly upon prayer for protection from thieves!

Please pray for those whose dispossession leads them to live in constant uncertainty and fear, and that effective help may reach them through Christian care and compassion.

CONTEMPLATION AND STRUGGLE
February 2002

FROM THE DAYS when I used to visit the Taizé Community in France, I recall the twin foci of their endeavours, described as contemplation and struggle. Young people especially seem to respond to their mode of prayer and worship with its distinctive chants, which feeds their engagement with a world that still knows little of the peace and harmony of God's kingdom.

Living in Malawi it is impossible to overlook that liturgy and life belong together. We are particularly fortunate here in having an excellent bimonthly magazine *The Lamp*, produced by Montfort Media since 1995, which addresses the many social, cultural and political issues facing the country. It is very much a child of Malawi's new democratic order. Under Dr Banda there was firm separation of Church and State, when religion was required to keep one's eyes raised to heaven, with never a downward nor a sideways glance at the world around. Our friend, bishop Patrick Kalilombe, found this to his cost when he attempted to introduce small parish communities into his diocese of Lilongwe. The authorities feared that they might discuss issues of governance and justice – and sent Kalilombe into exile for twenty years.

It is the Church's role not only to pray for secular authorities, but to be a partner in critical dialogue. There are still too many instances of corruption and mismanagement in Malawi which feature in *The Lamp*. Out of many such articles, one story must suffice, as related by Augustine Musopole, General Secretary of Malawi Council of Churches, in a recent edition:

> A long-serving and loyal civil servant reached retirement age, and was entitled to claim a lump-sum gratuity. Weeks passed by as he wrote, phoned and called, with increasing desperation. Finally, he was offered an advance in return for a 10% 'service charge'.

A new group of Christian laymen, 'The Voice of Micah', has emerged this year named after one of the outspoken Old Testament prophets. They too courageously detail some of the scams, great and small, that besmirch the name of this country. There is growing concern about the misspending of government funds and the widening gap between the rulers and their subjects. Yet, worryingly, members of the ruling party frequently allude to their intention to change the constitution so that their man (Bakili Muluzi) can remain in office as President for a third term.

However, Church and State are not necessarily set on the collision course of 1992, which in the end brought down Dr Banda's government. There is still sufficient goodwill to co-operate. A hopeful sign in February was the accord struck between the government and leaders of the main faith communities to collaborate more closely in the fight against HIV/AIDS through programmes of prevention and care. Both sides will 'continue to emphasise abstinence and mutual faithfulness as the best means of avoidance and prevention'. The Vice-President, an Anglican, has helpfully commented:

> I am proud of the work by Malawian and other theologians in developing pastoral-theological texts, which emphasize tolerance, love and compassion. While AIDS has no cure, it is possible to heal the spirit of people suffering from AIDS. We must acknowledge how vulnerable people are when they are sick. Many cannot find meaning in their suffering and lapse into despair, feeling worthless and unloved. The faith communities can give hope through emphasising that they are loved, that the spirit transcends the body, and that God is ready to welcome them to eternal life.

The fact that a leading politician can speak in those terms here in Africa reminds us that Western benefactors, while rightly being appalled at the squandering of resources, nevertheless have something to receive in return. What British politician could readily make such a public profession? Africans may not be saints, but in their struggles the place of 'contemplation' can still be acknowledged. The Churches are even invited to go to the heart of the matter, beyond the reach of politics and politicians.

The motto of *The Lamp* is drawn from Proverbs: 'It is better to light a lamp, than to curse the darkness.' So in the edition marking the centenary of the Catholic Church's presence in Malawi I was grateful to read the words of their retiring Archbishop:

I never wanted to be a bishop, and more than once refused. The one apostle that I admire most is Peter, a fisherman, a simple person who went as far as giving his life. We need to recapture the spirit of the first Christians. Let us be holy, let us love the faith like them, let us dedicate our life to the service of the Good News. Now I have reached the age when bishops retire from office. We have no pension, but I find myself completely free to do the pastoral work that was at the beginning of my vocation. I will live at the youth centre here in Blantyre, and I will continue serving the Church. That is what I love Like the apostles I will be a pastor travelling from village to village, repeating the story of Jesus and his loving Mother.

His words, the fruit of a lifetime's contemplation, touched me, and will, I trust, remind us all of how we can serve the struggles of our time.

Please pray for Malawi's leaders, that politicians and church representatives may continue to work together for the true welfare of their people.

Vwaza Marsh
One of the wildlife reserves, to the south of Nyika Plateau.
Hippos can be seen in the water.

THE MAIZE CRISIS
March 2002

THE MAIZE CRISIS is now at its peak. When crops were destroyed by heavy rains and floods a year ago, it was clear that last April's maize harvest would have a very poor yield, so that the 'hunger months' would begin much earlier than usual (families often have to cut back to one meal a day or less around the end of the calendar year, but this was already happening last September). Unbelievably, however, much of the country's strategic grain reserve was sold to Kenya last August, yet in November the main distributors were still telling the public that there was no problem. By January reserve supplies had become extremely low. Villagers queued in their hundreds at the Zomba depot – sometimes standing in heavy rain and sleeping out overnight – and were allowed to buy only a very meagre amount at three times the normal price. Some bribed the security guards and jumped the queue, but the rest were held back with iron bars. Finally our local depot shut down altogether. Elsewhere, such as Blantyre, profiteers who bought grain when the price was much lower remain in business making huge profits.

Despite this being the number one issue affecting everybody in the country, the main government newspaper carries virtually nothing on the crisis. There are no statements about any forthcoming relief to the situation, and certainly no apology for exacerbating the problems. Ministers are well-fed themselves, so why bother to offer explanations to the millions in such desperate plight? The severity of the famine is evidenced in the hospitals, which are packed with malnourished children and babies. In some places, people survive only by scavenging in the wild (one local doctor operated on a woman whose stomach was simply a mat of grass). There are rumours that South African grain is on its way, but it is also suggested that this is being re-routed through Botswana and Zambia to avoid the lorries being attacked and looted in Zimbabwe, where a similar, but chiefly man-made, food crisis obtains. Even when relief supplies have entered Malawi, internal distribution will then inevitably take several days.

Our college, which costs the equivalent of about £7,000 per month to run, started the new academic year with £370 in the bank. The main sending churches and synods in Malawi still owe considerable sums from the previous year. Even, therefore, if maize were plentiful it would not be easy to feed 100 students and their families. A great deal of the Principal's time is spent phoning and writing to the church officers in Malawi to pay their arrears and to send the funding each month as agreed by them at the regular college board meetings. Please pray for Dr Mwakandi in his unenviable task, which drove one of his predecessors to an early grave.

At least there is better news of the Songani Community Care Group. Help has come from many generous friends and church groups in England to enable the programme of feeding these orphans over the early months of 2002 to continue. Some rice is still locally available at the moment, so Mr Mpoya hired a lorry one day recently and set off in pouring rain determined to find it, reportedly in villages near Lake Chilwa. He was successful in buying 26 x 70kg sacks of rice – a fortnight's supply which cost roughly £330. As he returned, the lorry kept getting stuck in the muddy track, leaving no alternative but to unload the sacks in order to get the vehicle moving again. This whole operation had to be repeated several times over the return journey of 20 miles, so that the expedition lasted 12 hours in all. The rice was distributed the following day, and has proved so popular that a repeat has been requested; indeed, maize may remain unavailable.

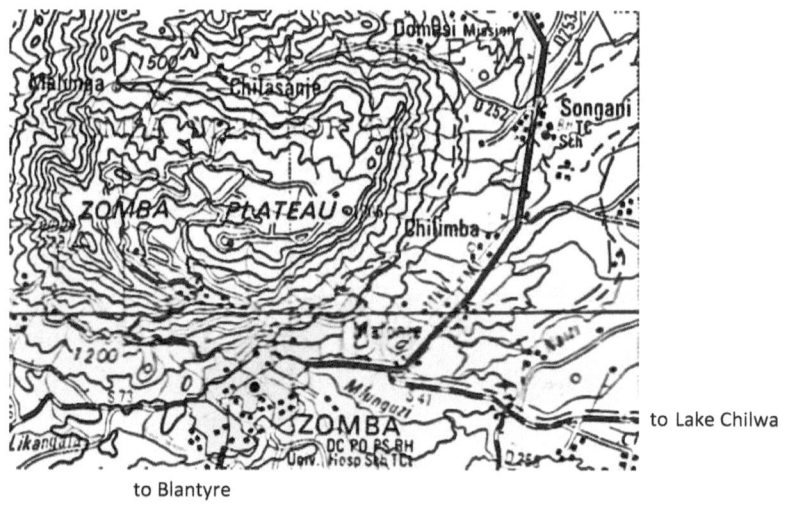

We hope that some prioritisation will be given to the orphans if and when imports of grain arrive in the country. The President's wife seems to have a keen interest in the care of orphans, of whom there are now nearly one million across the whole of Malawi. In response to a letter Sarah wrote to her late last year, she is coming to visit the project shortly. Please pray for Kennedy Mpoya and his helpers in the dedicated work that they are doing, and thank God for seeing them through thus far.

Despite the material worries, college has made a good start to the new academic year. We have eight new Anglican ordinands among the intake. They are for the most part unmarried and in their middle or late twenties. We rejoice that housing problems are on their way to being solved, with new accommodation both on the college campus and on our Anglican site further down Chirunga Road. Repairs to several of the older buildings are next on the agenda. Two new members of staff have also arrived, one from the Church of Scotland to teach theology, the other a Malawian recalled from Mozambique to teach Old Testament and Hebrew.

I remain as the only Anglican lecturer for the time being, but face additional responsibilities within the parish, at least until September when the priest who is nominally in charge should be returning from his studies abroad. We feel very sad for his family, who were evicted from the rectory by the churchwardens after he left, but at least the bishop has now intervened to restore them and pressed for an apology. Clergy here (no less than in England) can be subject to harassment, even by their own parishioners.

This year my focus with Anglican students is to be sacramental theology, along with some greater attention to their preparation for preaching. I am hoping that the staff will find time to review our teaching syllabus, in so far as it addresses or fails to address important local issues. Poverty, witchcraft and AIDS are among the most striking features of the Malawi landscape, and it may be that these have not been given adequate consideration within the overall college programme. (1) The issue of poverty is one that raises questions about the expectations that students may have for their future lifestyle and pattern of ministry, which are still largely based on inherited Western models. (2) The ubiquitous occurrence of witchcraft, and the universal fear of it, raises significant doubts about the relevance of some aspects of our syllabus, and whether we really prepare our students for mission in Malawi as it is today. (3) AIDS is ever with us, and while we have gone some way to meet its challenge, there remains a culture of embarrassment and silence on the subject.

Last September several staff members spent a week in Botswana at a conference organised by the World Council of Churches. The object was to help theological colleges address the many areas of life that relate to AIDS, with particular attention being given to different aspects of the curriculum – biblical, pastoral, catechetical and so on. This may already be bearing fruit in other colleges, but here, as all too often, it seems so far to have been regarded as little more than a shared holiday abroad with all expenses paid. Changes will no doubt eventually be introduced, but implementation even of unanimously agreed improvements is liable to take much longer than necessary.

On a personal note, we were glad to receive many Christmas cards, with (we suspect) still more yet to come. The hold-up now seems to lie more in Johannesburg than within Malawi. On the plus side, electronic communication is steadily improving within Malawi, and water, electricity and telephone have become much more reliable – despite occasional thefts of pipes and wires along the road sides. An attempt was even made to cut a high voltage overhead power line on the way to Blantyre, but the culprit – wholly ignorant of the danger – died from his burns.

Sadly we lost one of our two dogs in December, poisoned by a would-be intruder. The other dog was badly slashed by a panga knife across the mouth and throat, and needed fifteen stitches. Despite undoing her stitches two or three weeks later, Lily is well on the road to recovery. The garden, indeed the whole of the country, is looking green and leafy again, and we are glad to see the hill next to us, with its 'protected' woodland, luxuriating in growth after very fierce fires a few months ago.

So we are grateful for many mercies, and look forward to another year of God's surprising grace.

Please pray that supplies of maize may continue to reach those who are hungry, and for a good harvest in Malawi.

CHILD LABOUR
April 2002

FOR MANY YEARS the school-going population of Malawi has been affected by child-labour. A current estimate is that perhaps 250,000 children between the ages of 6 and 16 are involved. The numbers are increasing dramatically at present owing to the impact of AIDS and of inadequate food supplies in the villages.

In urban areas, particularly the two major cities of Blantyre and Lilongwe, employment in domestic service is engaging more and more young girls. Their remuneration is minimal, however, and prostitution is an increasingly frequent alternative. Indeed, newspaper cartoons appear regularly that lampoon the business community. Typically, girls are shown having a 'carpet' interview with their potential new boss. Such common activity is carried out in the apparent belief that young girls are risk-free sexual partners. As for boys, they flood into the towns as street-vendors. This very day in Zomba three of them have just been shot dead in a battle with the police. Almost any time they can be seen around the market or in the centre of town loading and offloading trucks, often shifting weights that are far too heavy, and thus incurring injuries which may last a lifetime.

In the rural areas, available manpower is being eroded by malnutrition and disease, with TB and cholera being especially rampant and seemingly on the increase. Against this should be set Malawi's impressive record for child immunisation, which is one of the best in Africa. The downside is that children are more available to take over adult jobs, particularly on tea or tobacco estates. Again, with most Malawians needing to grow most of their own food (as 'subsistence' farmers), children customarily do their share of work in the fields with other family members, alongside various domestic duties. By Lake Malawi, boys often prefer to fish than to attend school — a not unnatural inclination, yet actually the only option for those who are orphans or who have to look after a sick parent.

While free primary education is in theory provided across the country, the reality is that only a proportion of children carry on as far as standard 8. Even fewer attend secondary school where fees range from

1000 kwacha (roughly £10) per term for day schools, to perhaps 6000 kwacha for those who board. The latter is good value for money, but few can afford it. Poverty precludes many from even thinking about such further studies, while the high incidence of AIDS-related deaths among teachers means that the number available to work in schools is dropping far faster than those in training can replace them.

There are other factors too which inhibit the efforts of those (including the churches) who are concerned to promote life-skills among the young. Corruption is not unknown even in schools or among their suppliers. Thus, when a teacher has died, their name sometimes remains on the school pay roll – enabling the head-teacher to claim a salary on their behalf. Again, there is a well-rehearsed story concerning the construction of a new school. Invoices were passed at regular intervals to the government education department, and were duly paid. Eventually a high-ranking civil servant reckoned that with the work evidently nearing completion, a departmental visit was due to inspect the premises, so that arrangements could be put in hand for staff and pupil recruitment and an opening ceremony arranged. The site inspection was a shock, with nothing rising above the ground at all, despite the provision of several million kwacha.

When an extremely variable climate, giving rise to floods and droughts by turn, is thrown into the equation, and when expenditure by ministers and MPs on their own allowances is seen to run at unaffordable levels of luxury, it is understandable why some youngsters choose to make their own way in the world, seizing upon any available opportunities to keep themselves alive. One estimate is that there are 8000 street children living and sleeping rough in the main urban areas, hoping to escape hunger, poverty and family break-up – and yet seriously risking violence and sexual abuse. The gap between rich and poor in Malawi remains as high as anywhere in the world. Until justice begins to prevail, many of the social problems will continue unabated despite the best efforts of a growing number of charitable projects.

Please pray for the street children, and for youngsters who are exploited or abused.

A NEW DIOCESE
May 2002

AT THE BEGINNING OF MAY a new chapter began in the history of the Anglican Church here. A new diocese was born, making a total of four within Malawi (which in turn lies within the Province of Central Africa). The old diocese of Southern Malawi has split into two parts. Upper Shire is the name for the northerly half; the remainder continues to be known as Southern Malawi whose bishop James is shortly to move from Malosa to Blantyre, where the existing cathedral is to be found. Zomba parish is at the southern end of the new diocese, which stretches to Lake Chilwa in the east and Lake Malawi in the north.

At the same time our parish has grown, with the addition of Magomero, site of the first Anglican mission (1861) in Central Africa. The

book by Owen Chadwick called *Mackenzie's Grave* tells quite a lot about the early days of mission there. It lies about an hour's drive from Zomba. We went out one Sunday to welcome an old student, Fr Brighton Malasa, who has been placed there. There was a Malawian mix-up, so on that occasion we missed him. Nevertheless, it was very moving to celebrate mass in the open air under the trees, in the loop of the Namadzi River, with Mulanje mountain as a distant backdrop and Fr Burrup's cross and grave in the foreground. We return this coming Sunday to renew our acquaintance. Brighton is the first priest to be stationed at St Mackenzie's, as it is known, since the days of Fr Burrup 140 years ago. A new clergy house has been built, with solar panelling! At the moment there is a very small chapel dating back to the 1980s, but we hope a large church can soon go up. There are certainly plenty of Christians there, as in the nine or ten outstations it will also serve.

Meanwhile, our new diocese awaits the election of its first bishop, with the enthronement presently planned for 8th August. Choirs at St George's and our various daughter churches are beginning to practise in readiness. Sadly there is much controversy between different factions within the diocese about the new appointment, which may result in the process being delayed. This will not be the first time that such disputes have broken out within the Malawian church, although in the past they chiefly reflected the desire of Anglicans on Likhoma Island to maintain their dominant role.

Developments continue within college too. At last we have some Anglican students resident on our own site. Bishop James has found funds from an English trust to enable the building programme to continue and there is increasing support for the move towards independence. A North American diocese has also offered us a consignment of books for the library. The main concern is to improve pastoral and spiritual formation in our Anglican students, whereas our Presbyterian partners insist upon academic programmes at the expense of much else. Thus, a recent imposition has been the requirement that all students take two classes of Greek and two of Hebrew each week, where previously this was just an option for those who were suitably gifted. Apart from a simple introduction to Greek and Hebrew (including familiarity with their alphabets), sufficient to enhance understanding of biblical commentaries, for most of our students such further study is a waste of their time and unnecessary in the ministry they will exercise. It would preclude any room in the timetable for practical training in, say, youth work or AIDS counselling.

Out of 29 first year attempts last term to write a radio script on the subject of AIDS, it was by and large only the Anglican students who displayed a sense of compassion for its victims. Virtually all the others described the disease as God's scourge upon sinners (and this after considerable discussion in class reviewing a variety of different approaches). This attitude is being bred in our partner's churches before students ever reach us, but I was disturbed to find one staff member agreeing with this point of view in a sermon given recently in chapel. He implied that there is no possibility of salvation for those who have AIDS. It is sad that in many of these CCAP churches Sunday by Sunday the same message is handed out relentlessly, 'Obey God or he will punish you.' It is very hard indeed to get students with this mindset instilled in them from an early age ever to speak of God's love or forgiveness or to attempt some positive and hopeful guidance for Christian living in their sermons. In recent efforts for an Easter message (sic) the following themes were put forward:

Judas went and hanged himself.
Stop sinning and abide by God's rules.
We are all sinners.
Repent if you want to be with Jesus.
God's enemies go to hell.
Following God's rules.
Do you know what Hell's like?

I suspect that several of these suggestions would be more at home within a Muslim environment of hell-fire preaching and damnation.

A further disappointment is that our desire to stimulate the liturgy and to introduce new hymns has been vetoed, despite a staff agreement that such proposals were necessary and to be welcomed. The Principal informed us instead that the students' task was to practise only those hymns (seldom more than a dozen in rural communities) that their congregations would be likely to know already. Most of these are Chewa versions of Sankey revival songs from the late 19th century that feature storms, dark clouds, dismal prospects, thorns, deserts, toil, thunder, rocky steeps and the inevitable crimson tides. Their only redeeming feature lies in the way they are usually sung, with rich African harmonies. Ignorance of Chichewa can help one to participate in their singing a little more enthusiastically!

I have described our difficulties in some detail to illustrate why Anglicans are unhappy in this 'ecumenical' college, which we feel is not serving Malawi as well as it might. Our anticipated move is not because we lack the desire to cooperate. Our problem as Anglicans is that we are very much the lesser partners in a predominantly Presbyterian institution. It is difficult sometimes not to feel that we are outsiders. You will perhaps see that, as the only Anglican on the teaching staff this year, life can be pretty tough. But our own Anglican students are a great strength, as is the congregation at St George's, where we have very supportive friends.

Much more positively, it is good to report that the programme of seminars for which I am responsible has been going well, with good attendances including staff and students from the university and from St Peter's Catholic Seminary. We are shortly to have a final year Anglican student report on his research into the building of Likoma Cathedral in the early 1900s, followed by the distinguished Southern African economist Prof C. Chipeta discussing poverty reduction programmes in Malawi. We also anticipate hearing about the continuing difficulties of women who have given birth to stillborn babies – traditionally 'discarded' in some areas without proper burial – and of children suspected of being witches when their mothers failed to survive the trauma of their birth.

My own contribution has been to examine how witchcraft and divination feature in the Bible. They have featured several times in these monthly reports because of their prominence within Malawi. In fact, I have just completed the draft of a second book, under the provisional title *Mystery or Magic: Biblical Replies to the Heterodox*, which is likely to be published once again by Kachere Press, although not until next year.

Please pray for harmony and concord in the planned new developments, in both the dioceses concerned and within the college.

POVERTY ISSUES
June 2002

WE ARE VERY GLAD that the orphan feeding programme at Songani and surrounding villages ran successfully until the new harvest was ready. More often than not, local rice was purchased, as maize was in short supply. The distribution took place every second Saturday morning, when the children would arrive with their plastic bowls or bags to receive their allocation. Each child was given 5 kg of grain to last through the fortnight ahead. They would then depart, balancing their supplies carefully on their heads.

The number of orphans registered here continues to climb, and is now well past the 400 mark. At the same time, our craft training courses are expanding their scope. For example, there are hopes to add shoe mending skills, plus soap and candle making, later this year. One extremely useful project occurs at weekends, when perhaps 10 or 12 of the older boys go with the carpenter Mr Kuswele to Zomba Central Hospital to make mosquito mesh frames for all the windows there, which should significantly reduce the incidence of malaria contracted during hospitalisation. The boys have now reached their third ward, with many more to go. It is anticipated that their reward will be to possess a few tools of their own – but more importantly to have practical skills as a source of income. There are hopes of future employment for them locally making doors and window frames for the village huts. At Songani itself there is scope to build cow sheds to accommodate several milking cows. Funding is being sought for the latter project and for a maize mill, which would also engage the brick-laying team in its construction. Such a mill would be able to generate cash for the community, apart from being a convenient asset to the village. We gather that Mr Vladi's tin group find ready sales for their buckets and saucepans.

In addition to the care provided, and the courses offered, SCCG has a couple of ample gardens for growing its own maize. One yielded a very good harvest in April, about 16 x 50 kilogramme sacks. The other promised even better, but was stripped of all its cobs by thieves. This started to happen on a wide scale in other places too, and forced villagers to harvest their maize before it was properly ripe. Others who were desperate for food ate their crops while still green, and so have little left for the months that lie ahead. Others again were too weak at the end of last year even to prepare their land and to sow any crop. Hence starvation threatens on a larger scale than in the previous year. There will be much hunger later in 2002, and of course into the first quarter of 2003. We understand that the British media have already drawn attention to the looming problems. With drought having affected the whole region, Malawi cannot rely entirely upon her neighbours for the large consignments of relief aid that will certainly be needed. There are reports that the UN Famine Relief Programme is prepared to replenish Malawi's strategic grain reserves – under strict conditions of accountability.

The organiser at Songani, Kennedy Mpoya, is a good Christian and a hard worker who cares for his people. Currently he is buying in sacks of grain in local markets in readiness for the crisis in store. Heartfelt thanks go to family and friends in England who have made this possible through their generous donations and their continuing prayers. Be assured that the storage sheds at Songani are now properly weather-proof, rat-proof, and burglar-proof! Many or the orphans have also been 'weather-proofed' for this particularly cold winter. It has been possible to provide them with proper blankets to replace the sacks they used previously.

Carolyn, the Malawian orphan for whom we care, has been busy with further typing courses, and hopes to be selected for a one year course at Soche Technical College in Blantyre soon. It has been so distressing for her to learn of deaths occurring frequently within her own extended family that she has now come to see her future in secretarial work, rather than in nursing. Her one aim is to improve her qualifications, and she works very hard to achieve this. She is a great help to us in the house with her cooking, and has become an expert farmer. In her small garden here (1/27th of a hectare) she produced two sacks of maize, which is the top target rate for those using hybrid seed and fertiliser. When she is ready to leave us to live independently, we know of a pre-ordination candidate who might benefit from taking her place – a former Muslim rejected by his family who is aiming to gain his Malawi certificate of education before going to college.

Please pray for less fortunate children who receive little or no care.

AFRICANS ABROAD
July 2002

TWO YOUNG PEOPLE, each having completed their secondary education, have recently travelled to England from Malawi. The young man spent a successful term as a teaching assistant in a school, but at Christmas the word came through that he was undergoing severe mental dissociation. His memory had gone, and he could scarcely express himself. Naturally, his parents felt that one of them should fly immediately to be at his side regardless of the expense entailed. Two weeks later I met his mother in Zomba, when she reported all was well, although her son was moving to stay with her sister in London and was looking for new work. What had happened was that someone at a Christmas party had laced her son's drink with a potent cocktail of drugs, which had induced the mental breakdown.

The young lady, who was taking a one-year course in a college in the home counties, has now decided of her own volition to abandon her studies (which she was enjoying) because she felt wholly alienated by the lifestyle of others on the course. One of these was the girl with whom she shared a flat. She had not been prepared for the relentless obsession with sex, drink and drugs, which intruded upon her own privacy to the extent that she was left with little time or space to be herself. She had not found any fellow students with whom any normal (and mutually respectful) friendship was possible, so has returned to Africa to apply for a local course and to live in a place where she expects behaviour to be less barbaric.

'Two swallows don't make a summer', of course, but I did feel ashamed of the experiences received at the hands of my compatriots. Such abandonment of moral values in England cannot be charged simplistically to any single cause, however much in a culture of blame such a temptation exists: yet this is still considered, as many Africans have been taught, 'Christian' England, and the disjunction between the epithet and the reality surely needs clearer recognition by the churches both at home and abroad.

A decade or two ago when we were serving in Lesotho it was not uncommon for us to come across white South Africans who, having sold up in the face of spiralling violence and gone to live in their mother country, had been equally as shocked as the two young students. They complained not so much of drink and drugs but of what they termed 'a declining moral decency' in England, citing the ubiquity of pornography and the degradation of much television. As a result they too had returned home, to face again the iniquities of apartheid. 'For years and years,' they said, 'we've been lectured on how unChristian it is to collude, even if reluctantly, with such a corrupt social order. We recognize the validity of such remarks – but we were deceived into thinking that the Western world held the morally high ground. What price social justice if there is no dignity in life and nothing sacred left?'

Such comments need also to be heeded by those who are now active in aid programmes, or who campaign for Third World debt remission, or who pray for the development of fair trade. Jesus' concern was not limited to material well-being, important though that is. He knew that 'man does not live by bread alone'; he came that we might have life 'in all abundance'. That certainly includes good health and education, food, shelter and whatever is spelt out in any listing of human rights – but there is so much more as well.

The present danger is that spiritual impoverishment in the West may be exported, along with aid and trade, to countries such as Malawi. What is food and plenty if people's hearts and minds are captured by a mood of materialism, or are violated by videos (readily available even in rural communities here, where car batteries provide the power), or imprisoned in unbridled individualism? Traditional ways are still much in evidence here, but there is a steady tide of Western culture washing over the country. One form of enslavement (the bonds of debt) may well be replaced in time by another (the culture of discontent). What else does modern advertising and much commerce feed upon?

Thus, while questions are constantly being asked of us here in Zomba, by partner churches and other outside bodies (recently, the World Council of Churches), as to what we are doing to combat AIDS, corruption, poverty and environmental degradation, it is reasonable that in return Third World countries should be told how First World Christians are tackling the moral deficit in their own back garden.

A Malawian Muslim, recently arrived in the UK to serve as an imam in Leicester, was interviewed about the rise in Muslim extremism which resorts to terrorist activities. 'Why,' he was asked, 'do you think – as a moderate yourself – that so many of your co-religionists are now opposed to the West?' In reply, he simply drew attention to the spread of pornography, to drugs, to anti-social behaviour, to the apparent lack of accepted moral teaching ... and then suggested that, although the West's acquisition of a disproportionate share of the world's natural resources certainly rankled, the greater affront lay in the perception of morally and spiritually bankrupt nations presuming to dictate principles to other countries and to interfere in their internal affairs.

Students often raise related issues in our ethics classes. 'What about the war on terror?' is a frequent question, as is 'What about the threatened invasion of foreign places?' Although these are complex matters, my response usually includes a reference to Jesus' teaching about removing beams from one's own eyes as a necessary part of the process.

Yet despite the failure of human attempts to measure up to the demands of the Gospel, the churches in the West do, I believe, have a calling to continue sharing their faith with peoples elsewhere – and that may include sharing other values too that are consonant with Christianity. That does not preclude a reciprocal response: perhaps one should begin to identify aspects of African faith and culture which could be exported – much to the spiritual and moral benefit of the West?

Please pray that churches across the world may witness faithfully and prophetically to their own spiritual and moral teachings.

VENERATION OF ANCESTORS

August 2002

DINIS SENGULANE, Anglican Bishop of Lebombo in Mozambique, offered a helpful insight some ten years ago into what brought liturgy alive for Africans:

> When liturgy takes into account children, the young, adults, the old, the departed, spiritual beings (whether regarded as angels or demons), rain and environment, national leaders, heaven and hell, houses and fields, colour and movement, gestures and symbols, then it is dealing with what concerns African peoples.

Although African traditional religion (ATR) does not always measure up to Christian expectations, a heartening trend – at least within several Catholic Bishops' Conferences – has been to seek some positive appraisal of its strengths i.e. those that are potentially compatible with Christian faith. Most African churches would endorse the following as likely candidates:

Belief in the afterlife
A sense of mutual dependence and belonging
Spiritual cults catering for the emotional needs of people
Meaningful use of symbolism
Belief in the existence of spirits
Bonds between the living and deceased relatives
A strong sense of community
Prayer to ancestors in times of crisis
Belief in the supreme God and Creator
Sacred shrines
Initiation rites at different stages of life
Times of festival and celebration such as harvest
The importance of family and extended family
Traditional prayers and titles of God
The inseparable link between life and faith
Rites of purification for individuals and communities

One conclusion that might be drawn is that, since religious celebrations are understood as mediating harmony between people, and between them and the invisible powers, so the Eucharist can surely be seen as a fulfilment of African hopes when considered as a rite of healing both for individuals and for the community as a whole.

Clearly, though, there are particular themes whose inclusion in the list above is more debatable. Of these, it is 'prayer to ancestors' that comes under most scrutiny. The Congolese Catholic theologian Kabasele Lumbala notes how, at least in *traditional* African culture, interaction between the living and the dead is fundamental:

> The interdependence of the members of a Bantu clan is such that an individual receives life through the ancestors and is unthinkable apart from them. As the individual grows in life, communion with the ancestors intensifies, and this intensification has an impact on the other members of the clan.

In interpreting this claim, it must be remembered that the term 'ancestor' does not simply mean 'any forebear' but principally (although not exclusively) one who has lived a worthy life and died a natural life, who was blessed with offspring and provided for them. This begins to suggest a certain rapprochement between African recourse to the ancestors and Christian veneration of saints. Yet we can observe that what the church proposes in its calendar of saints is a widening of the sense of family. For Christians, our ancestors may include blood relatives, but more importantly they are those who have gone before us as our brothers and sisters in the faith. So a narrow tribalism is being challenged from the perspective of Christ's universal love. In fact, he may be considered our supreme Ancestor. His words, addressed to his own family, are relevant here:

> He replied, 'Who are my mother and my brothers?' And looking around on those who sat about him, he said, 'Here are my mother and my brothers! Whoever does the will of God is my brother, and sister, and mother.'

The distinction (not always articulated clearly) between worthy and unworthy ancestors is perhaps mainly concerned with the question as to who may or may not be expected to have the welfare of their descendants at heart – rather than Jesus' criterion of doing or not doing God's will.

There are also assumptions being made about the status of the departed which have been scrutinised more thoroughly in the Bible than in ATR. In ancient Hebrew belief, departed spirits lived but a shadowy and feeble existence in Sheol (or the Pit). It was at the later time of the Maccabaean martyrs when, probably influenced by Near Eastern thinking elsewhere, the idea of resurrection as divinely given compensation for their earthly sacrifice began to take hold. This was not necessarily achieved at the moment of death: a period of waiting, followed by God's judgement 'on the last day' when the good would be rewarded and the bad punished, was also envisaged. The same pattern seems to have been the earliest belief of Christians following the thoroughly attested resurrection of Christ himself. Paul, for example, initially writes of departed Christians as being 'asleep'. Later, however, when envisaging the possibility of his own demise by execution, he speaks of going to be 'with the Lord'. Certainly, when the book of the Apocalypse was written a few decades further on, it is accepted that there will be a 'fast stream' to heaven comprising outstanding heroes of the faith, such as Mary herself and the Christian martyrs.

So when, in a recent article in the Malawian magazine *The Lamp*, Augustine Musapole can write:

> Africans believe and therefore know that the human spirit continues to exist beyond the grave.

it is certainly necessary for the Church to point out (1) that such certain knowledge is only evidenced by Jesus' own resurrection and (2) that too many assumptions should not be made about the state of a departed person i.e. whether or not they are necessarily as accessible as the saints and martyrs are believed to be. Christians for these reasons should not endorse the drumming, dancing and hand-clapping that is traditionally carried out by 'healers' to make contact with the ancestors.

A suitably cautious and nuanced approach is found in the Roman Missal that was sanctioned some years ago for Zaire (as it was then known). The invocation of saints as proposed there allows for the inclusion of certain ancestors among their number, provided the qualification 'seeking God with sincerity' is noted:

Let us unite ourselves with all who, even though they had not known Christ in their lifetime, have however sought God with a sincere heart. With God's help they have accomplished God's will, and are now with God.

I ought not to conclude without mentioning the tension that now exists between, on the one hand, the perpetuation of Africa's valued traditions and, on the other, the need to adjust to a fast-changing global world. Modern developments and ideologies do not always sit comfortably with the African's traditional expectations and his world-view. But when the modern world leaves people desperately behind to face varieties of suffering and deprivation, it is natural that they will cling to any remedy that promises some respite, including the customs and beliefs of ATR. Hence, if the main-stream or mission churches neglect these traditions, there will be even more African Initiated Churches (AICs) springing up that in a whole variety of ways will seek to baptise them as Christian practices.

Even so, there are those, such as Fr Benezet Bujo, who can speak of such inculturation as 'a pompous irrelevance':

> African culture, like all other cultures, is not static but participates in the process of evolution. The search for the genius of African culture runs the risk of invading the Church of today with aspects of African life of the past which may today impede progress or which have, by their nature, become redundant.

Please pray for wisdom in discerning what is of true and lasting value, both in traditional ways of life from the past, and in the many influences that now infiltrate Malawi from elsewhere.

FISHING TACTICS
September 2002

LAKE MALAWI IS FAMOUS for its fish, especially *chambo* and *kapinga*, or the smaller *usipa* (rather like whitebait). Until twenty years ago, these were caught in abundance; but now – with a rapidly rising population and the pressure on all food resources – the fishermen compete fiercely with each other. Among the northern Tonga people (as one of my students found in his research) there has been a wholesale recourse to magic and witchcraft to boost the catches. Charms, made of crushed bones and herbal ingredients, are positioned on different parts of the fishing gear to attract and hold the fish, but also to ward off the evil powers directed by other fishermen. Resort is made to witchdoctors as well as to priests and ministers of religion, in fact to anyone who can bring spiritual resources to bear, either to attract fish into the nets or to fight the spells that may prevent them getting there. When a catch is landed it has become necessary for the fisherman to eat at least one of the fish he has caught in order to demonstrate publicly that no ill effects will ensue i.e. that no competitor has succeeded in poisoning them. It remains something of a dilemma for Christian ministers to know how far they should allow themselves to be drawn into this competitive situation: with whom, and for what, should they offer prayer?

Almost every Wednesday afternoon, when we discuss in college the pastoral experiences of ordinands who have been out on placement, tales such as those reported from the lake shore are commonplace. Sorcery is alive and kicking in Malawi, despite a history of well over 100 years of Christian missions and a churchgoing attendance reckoned at around 75% of the nation. Nor is it simply the non-churchgoers who patronise the witchdoctors. Most priests will be familiar with children brought to baptism with charms already hung about their waists or their necks, usually placed there by grandparents for 'extra protection'. While the rule is that these must certainly be removed for any baptism to take place (after having explained that we have complete faith in the power of Christ to defend us against all evil), it is inevitable that many such charms will be reinstated once out of sight of the priest.

Indeed, many of our Christians live in fear of whatever magic may be directed against them. A prominent member of my own congregation has been in remission of spinal cancer for over a year, but there is now a strong indication that it has returned. The symptom is paralysis of the legs, yet without the sophisticated equipment found in Western hospitals the cause cannot definitely be diagnosed. He himself first noticed the reversion after an acrimonious meeting at a church secondary school, and – putting two and two together – deduced that someone there had 'prayed against him' and placed him under a curse. The key to this unlikely conclusion lies in the school's location, adjacent to the diocesan headquarters. As one of our churchwardens he has sided with the faction opposing the newly elected bishop, and interprets his own ill health within the context of this ongoing dispute, which is increasingly poisoning the atmosphere with unwarranted accusations of occult dealing.

It is clear from the history of witchcraft, which only began to die out in England after 1500 years of Christianity and even now is making a resurgence along with other irrational beliefs and practices, that it peaks at times of social stress, and is associated with distrust and jealousy. And if so, Africa today, with its frequent famines, its droughts and floods, its falling life expectancy due to tribal struggles and the impact of AIDS, is a prime location where such uncertainty can play havoc with people's minds. A South African researcher, to give a different example, was able to demonstrate clearly that resort to witch-finders peaked in certain areas as the pressures and upheavals of apartheid increased. Sadly, the accusing finger points too readily to those least able to defend themselves – children, the mentally handicapped, those already unpopular because they are in some way different.

What is the answer? Well, we preach week in and week out of the love of God, and of our faith as one of trust and confidence in him. And yet, it seems that in Europe it was not so much the Christian Church that eradicated fears of witchcraft as the rise of science, which began to suggest that nature could be understood and indeed controlled. Does then science, rather than faith, hold the key?

I have learnt since being in Malawi (1) that scientific solutions to African predicaments are worth nothing without a commitment of love and a patient readiness to adapt to the constraints of the African situation, but also (2) that the African's perception of spiritual forces at work, alongside the material factors, is a deep biblical truth often neglected in the west. Coming to Malawi has challenged me to reappraise aspects of Christian teaching which I had previously discounted – so these themes are explored in the new book mentioned previously, *Mystery or Magic: Biblical Replies to the Heterodox*. Nothing in our college library seems to deal adequately with such issues, which are of pressing concern.

Please pray for the victims of other people's fear and suspicion, for those who promote better understanding of life's predicaments, and for the churches' abiding witness to Christ's ultimate victory.

When fish become scarce and crops fail, Malawians turn to plants and roots growing wild that are both less palatable and less nourishing to help ward off the pangs of hunger.

In early spring (shortly upon us), even in times of plenty, they also look forward to enriching their diet in ways that are unfamiliar to most Westerners viz. by frying some of the insects that are then 'in season'.

Unlike some of the roots, these are very tasty and full of protein. In taxonomic terms they are not too far removed from shrimps. An entomologist speaking to the Zomba branch of the Wildlife Association suggested that, although over 12,000 different forms of insect life had so far been identified in Malawi, as many again might yet await discovery. Only a tiny percentage, one imagines, are edible.

At this time of the year *inswa*, the swarms of flying ants, are popular. In earlier months varieties of crickets, grasshoppers, locusts and caterpillars are also favoured.

THE HUNGER MONTHS RESUME
October 2002

DOWN AT COLLEGE Sarah has been kept just as busy with the ordinands' wives, helping them with English and the various handicrafts that they do. Further afield a watchful eye has been kept on the Songani orphan project, knowing that many families in the participating villages will soon run short of food. Last year's hunger was widespread, with some people too weak even to plant crops for this year. It also meant that this year's maize harvest was often eaten while still green and much was stolen from the fields. At Songani it was agreed that the feeding programme to cover the hunger months leading up to the next harvest (April 2003) would need to start early again, as it did in 2001. This in turn has meant that maize and rice have to be purchased regularly from the local markets so long as it remains available. Weekly trips to do so started in fact back in May, since when prices have steadily increased but at least for the present now seem more stable.

Buying and storing grain is more complicated than might sound at first. Often, one is not buying complete sacks (as from a government depot) but negotiating patiently with a number of different vendors in a village market for the contents of their plastic basins. On top of the transport that has to be arranged, the grain has to be thoroughly dried on its return before being mixed with acteric dust to deter weevils and placed in sacks. In the storage sheds planking has had to be arranged to allow good circulation of air. Finally, a watchman has had to be employed, as food thefts (and much other crime) are now common in the villages. At the time of writing, we have grain to last until February, with the following month or two still needing to be covered.

Although we hope these local orphans and their guardians will survive until the April harvest, there are probably many elsewhere who will not. Lack of food of course accentuates all the other problems faced in this country and makes people so much less able to fight disease. People living with HIV/AIDS need your special prayers at this time.

Despite his failure to provide Malawians with the basics of life such as health care, food security, and freedom from both local crime and high level corruption, the President (Bakili Muluzi) still seems bent on staying in office beyond his statutory two terms. When the present constitution was agreed in the previous decade, there was almost universal agreement not to allow another Life-President such as Kamuzu Banda, who had ruled increasingly despotically for nearly thirty years. In the middle of the year an unconstitutional edict was issued by Muluzi to the police, instructing them to disperse any public discussions of the issue. When I heard from the verger at St George's that armed police were stationed on our premises, I headed at once for the divisional headquarters to see the police chief. Fortunately – after an uncomfortable hour with him – I emerged safe and sound, and the police were afterwards withdrawn from church. My aim was to remind him that peaceful public gatherings are written into the constitution, which the police have a specific duty to uphold. Sadly, there has been much more recently a student protest down at Chancellor College, where a student was shot in the back and killed when running away from the police line. We also encounter not a few corrupt traffic policemen when travelling on the main road into Blantyre. They invent specious reasons for imposing an on-the-spot fine, and can be intimidating at times.

We have both remained in good health, although I underwent minor surgery in July, when a hammer toe was strightened. The surgeon was from England, a very dedicated doctor whose aim is to open a purpose-built children's hospital in Blantyre, which will be a 'first' for Malawi. The pre-medical check took place in the washroom of a local cafe rather than in Zomba Hospital: the doctor thought it would be more hygienic! It took fully eight weeks to recover from the operation, but friends in Zomba were very kind in lending books to be read during the period of immobility. Fortunately healing was well advanced by mid August when our daughter Patricia came out with a friend for a short holiday and we were able to get out and about to some of the lovely places in Malawi.

It was encouraging to see other visitors and tourists around too. Although Malawi has much to offer those from overseas, it is generally considered too far off the beaten track. The situation in Zimbabwe has of course impacted badly upon tourism here and we hardly ever see overlanders trekking through Zomba as we did a couple of years ago. There is, however, a steady flow of youngsters from UK schools or universities who come here for voluntary service (for example, under the auspices of Africa Venture). Usually their time is spent teaching English in the secondary schools. Such experience will surely contribute to better international understanding in the future.

Carolyn, the orphan whom we have taken under our wing, is now 22. She will remain here in charge of the house when we go on furlough after the end of term. She failed to get a place at Soche Technical College, probably because government cutbacks meant that fewer places were on offer. (We cannot help noticing that despite the cutbacks members of parliament voted to double their own salaries.) Instead, Carolyn has kept busy on typing and book-keeping courses and is learning short-hand. She hopes to be ready to find a secretarial job next year.

Once again, we're so grateful for the support we receive from partners in the UK and for all who have assisted the emergency feeding programmes. Life can be stressful here at times, even apart from the political and economic troubles, but we recognise that alongside the difficulties there are many blessings for which to be thankful and many warm-hearted friends and colleagues.

While we are on leave in November and December, we shall be seeing our son Gabriel and his family in California, where they have been living since July. Fortunately, our email works reliably and allows us to download photographs of the family, including pictures of Chloe our granddaughter. So we keep in touch and stay up to date. There will also be some deputation work for USPG before Christmas, visiting some of you, our supporters, in the various parishes.

Please pray for young people in Malawi looking for jobs or for further training.

COMING SOON
November 2002

THE GOOD NEWS is that the bishops in Malawi have decided that training for Anglican ordinands in Zomba should go ahead on an independent basis as soon as is practicable. I am currently involved with a small planning group, which includes Malawian Anglicans with good experience in both finance and building design. Whereas the bishops had hoped to launch the new college in January 2003, it is clear that this early date is unrealistic and will more likely be 2005. However, a name has already been decided. It will be the Leonard Kamungu Theological College (LKTC), named after the first Malawian to be ordained to the priesthood, by Bishop Hine in 1909 in the newly built St Peter's cathedral on Likoma Island. Kamungu died in 1913 after pioneering work in what is now Zambia and his feast day in the provincial calendar is 27 February.

The setting of LKTC is outstanding. It has beautiful views of Zomba mountain, and is located half way between our present college (ZTC) and the University of Malawi, whose library will become available to our students. Until recently the site was occupied by the main contractors working on Mulunguzi Dam. They rented it for several years from the diocese of Southern Malawi, and their offices and storage facilities are now being made habitable for residential and educational purposes. More money needs to be spent on these conversions than had initially been projected, as the contractors failed to fully observe the conditions of their rental agreement in terms of the buildings they erected. One open large barn will eventually become a chapel in the very centre of the campus. By January it should be possible for a few single students to swell the numbers already in residence. There are three staff houses almost ready now and it is envisaged that in due course there will be 24 students (two per year from each of the four dioceses in Malawi) together with 3 or 4 residential staff, a college secretary, and visiting lecturers.

Several Malawian priests are currently studying for higher degrees in the UK, USA, and South Africa, while one colleague will next year complete his doctorate here in Zomba. So by 2005 there should be some well qualified Anglicans to call upon. I have prepared illustrative weekly and termly timetables which show how, with a smaller staff than ZTC, it should be feasible to cover the syllabus and to continue preparing students for their UNIMA diploma – or even perhaps for a degree.

It has been difficult at times to persuade some committee members not to set their hopes too high about the level of facilities such as computers and vehicles. Those who have studied abroad carry images in their mind of well-equipped college campuses, and seem to imagine limitless funding being available for LKTC. (One of our present Anglican students sees an affluent lifestyle as his entitlement upon ordination, and is currently demanding a motor car as a perk of the job!) More realistically Sarah has plans for 'greening' the site with cuttings from our own garden, so at least it should be possible to transform what is presently a barren lorry park into a pleasant environment at minimal cost.

I am glad to say that the final year students, whose personal research projects I supervise, have achieved good standards and made several excellent seminar presentations during their last term. In interpreting the significance of New Testament teaching for Malawian life today, diverse passages were explored thoroughly and sensitively, giving rise to lively discussion. Themes included:

- the use of charms within Tonga villages
- agrarian ethics for Malawi
- a critique of popular evangelistic campaigns
- suffering in the work of ministry
- missiological aspects of liturgical language

The number of such BD (Bachelor of Divinity) candidates will be slightly less in 2003 but their quality and diligence promises to remain just as high.

Within the Board of Theological Studies, staff from the different constituent colleges help to examine each other's students and my impression is that Zomba Theological College maintains standards that compare more than favourably with the others, among whom one sometimes detects too much memorising of lecture notes and a lack of independent reading and thinking. This year I was asked to be the second marker for the optional Catholic canon law paper. While my detailed knowledge of the subject is limited, I was at least able to check the coherence of the answers given, and to give credit for clear presentation and good English!

Although my own teaching thus far has been mainly New Testament work, next year I have offered to help out with some Old Testament classes. Our main Old Testament lecturer is moving away to concentrate on Bible translation, while his colleague died earlier this year. No replacement has yet been found for either of them, perhaps because among academically able ministers and priests there is a noticeable tendency for higher degrees to be pursued in development studies or Malawian church history rather than in core biblical and doctrinal subjects. It will be important in the future for the balance to be corrected. Meanwhile, versatility remains the name of the game!

Please pray for those now engaged in paving the way for the long-anticipated independent Anglican college to become a reality in just over a year's time.

SEASONAL MEDITATIONS
December 2002

For Advent

'BE ON YOUR GUARD, stay awake; you never know when the time will come.'

Perceptions of time vary with each culture. In Western society people are encouraged to plan ahead, to be at least one step in front of time, to forestall its possible depredations. Recognizing that life is a chapter of accidents we insure against the unforeseen, trying to secure ourselves against whatever the future may choose to throw in our direction. There is a marked contrast in Africa where the issue is not tomorrow or the next day, but survival today – for indeed 'each day has troubles enough of its own'. Any longer term perspective seems often to be of secondary concern.

So the challenge of the Advent message is relative to the context in which it is heard. In the West it is necessary to wake up to the realization that we cannot insulate ourselves from the impact of God's future, whatever that may be. He has plans which may be very different from our own. To stress our own security may be to exclude God from our lives. At any time he may come to thwart our ambitions, if we are not alert to his deep purposes. Therefore we must learn to live closer to him day by day, taking perhaps less 'thought for the morrow.'

In Africa, however, the longer view is needed – the sense that God created the world and us human beings for maturity and growth, so that little by little we come to his intended fruition. In this process it should be recognised that each individual has a vital part to play, and that there must be a common commitment to work and pray for God's kingdom to come 'on earth as it is in heaven.' Where Westerners need the radical challenge of Christian alternatives, Africans need a dimension of hope that will encourage them against all odds to go on trusting a God whose love is stronger than death – indeed, to believe on the most difficult days that tomorrow will actually arrive, and that the strength to face it will come too.

For Christmas

'HE WAS NOT THE LIGHT, but was sent to bear witness to the light.'

Many times it is stressed in the Gospels that John the Baptist was not himself the Christ. His role was rather to prepare the way for one greater than himself. This is a word for those of us who are Christian leaders. When a new priest arrives in a parish, perhaps there are some who see him as their saviour, the one who will revive their fortunes. Perhaps the priest himself cherishes a messianic role? Or can this be true of some bishops? Do church leaders imagine that they are in control, and must therefore impose their plans and ideas upon others? Hopefully, the triumphalism that has raised its head too frequently in the recent past will subside, and more biblical concepts of the Christ will re-emerge: the lowly one, born in a stable, buried in a tomb, whose kingdom 'is not of this world.'

In the missionary context, triumphalism is out of place. Indeed, for good reason the phrase 'mission partner' is my current designation. Today in Africa expatriate workers receive a warm welcome, because they are perceived as able to access resources – funds, skills, and supplies. There has always been a possibility for missionaries to be seen as gods. Paul and Barnabas were once addressed in this fashion, but they were firm in insisting upon a humbler role. An important dimension of partnership, sometimes overlooked, is that of 'empowerment', drawing out and encouraging the possibly untapped potential of the people whom they serve. Missionaries need to bear witness to the light that guides others as well as themselves.

In practice today, this can sometimes mean denying people's hopes and expectations – not, of course, refusing to share resources with them, but when necessary focusing upon the greater gifts and blessings that belong to our Christian calling. In Zomba it would be easy to get sidetracked from my role as a teacher and a mentor for ordinands into becoming an administrator, fundraiser, or relief organizer. People's practical needs are very great, and the disparity between our advantages and those of the average Malawian is evident every day. Nevertheless, the Church's prime task here is to address the underlying beliefs and attitudes which can nullify even the best efforts of those who work to promote people's welfare. What use, for example, are condoms in an AIDS crisis if they encourage more widespread promiscuity and the breakdown of family life? How far can vocational training succeed if it is bedevilled by people's jealousy of others' progress? At a time of rapid social change, many feel threatened and afraid: the spectacle of apparently omni-competent outsiders alleviating their plight does not necessarily affirm the dignity, nor enhance the existing gifts, of those being helped. There are underlying needs that may not be addressed at all. At root, each one deserves more, that is, knowledge of the love of God revealed in Jesus Christ. He is the one 'who though he was rich became poor for our sakes', to heal us, forgive us, and uplift us. All a missionary can really hope to do is to witness to that liberating compassion.

For Epiphany

'WE HAVE SEEN HIS STAR in the east, and have come to worship him.'

Symbolically the magi represent the nations of the world, and by medieval times the tradition had grown that one of the kings must be portrayed as an African. What gifts does he then offer to our Lord? This is not a question that has always been asked, since for some it was axiomatic that any society located beyond the bounds of Christendom was pagan in character. Seen in that light their task was to eradicate whatever was contrary to the gospel, rather than to build upon the work God might have done before their own arrival.

Now that the days of Christendom are over, a revaluation becomes possible. Part of the missionary task in the West is to ask searching questions about our own society, and the ways it has reverted into paganism. If a Christian critique could once be applied to African culture, should it not now be applied as stringently to Britain and America? But again, perhaps in the past what was overlooked in Africa were some of its existing spiritual strengths, already gifted there by God. Maybe today, in the face of moral decay at home, we can appreciate better what Africa has to bring before the Lord.

Here, briefly, are a couple of suggestions. Malawi advertises itself as 'the warm heart of Africa', and this is an indication both of the friendliness of the people, but also of their joy and resilience. Even in times of disaster or crippling hardship, this is notable in their worship, which has a vitality sometimes lacking in more affluent settings. In these difficult days, when death is stalking the land, with nearly a million children now orphaned, it is hard to imagine how Britain could cope with such a situation. But a second characteristic is helping to see Malawi through, namely, the strong sense of family. Of course, the social fabric is under immense strain, but without the support of the extended family, caring for both young and old in their need, it would collapse altogether. Neither characteristic was a missionary import, but it may well be that, baptised into Christ's service, they are gifts that should now be exported elsewhere.

Please pray for a growing sense of partnership between the churches of the different continents.

No Room at the Inn?

When I am thirsty, I turn on the tap.
  When I am thirsty, I walk to the well.
When I want food, I load up a supermarket trolley.
  When I want food, I see what I've grown in the field.
When I am sick, I drive round to the surgery.
  When I am sick, they carry me miles to the clinic.
When I need clothes, I look out for the fashions.
  When I need clothes, I hunt through the pile in the market.
When I am lonely, I text or phone my friends.
  When I am lonely, I pray God to give me back my family.
When I've finished for the day, I watch a film.
  When I've finished for the day, it's pitch dark everywhere.
When I'm hungry, I have a snack.
  When I'm hungry, I stay hungry.

YEAR 2003

Martial Eagle
Not uncommon in Malawi, and larger than the African Fish Eagle
(which we also sighted more than once)

Firing bricks
Villagers mould their own bricks from clay soil
before stacking them as shown for the firing process.

Re-thatching and re-coating
New grass is collected each year for re-thatching.
The walls, both inside and out, as well as the floor, are also re-coated annually,
using a mixture of soil and cow dung (which hardens like cement).

RESILIENCE AND JOY

January 2003

DURING OUR FURLOUGH back in England, we saw many friends and supporters in a number of parishes. In December, we travelled quite a lot on deputation visits, seeing old faces and new in the counties of Derbyshire, Leicestershire, Northamptonshire, Cambridgeshire, Somerset and Dorset. It was particularly heartening to see young priests doing excellent work in a number of different parishes and to learn that bishop Keith Newton has adopted our work as an official project for his See of Richborough. Altogether, we gave about ten formal or informal presentations. It was tiring work with the attendant travel, especially as we were both suffering the after-effects of throat infections. But there were rewarding conversations with a number of individuals who had aspirations to serve one day as missionaries themselves. Several parishes indicated that they had just become supporters of this project –so a warm welcome if this is the first newsletter to reach you.

Then of course we also caught up with our own family. We spent two weeks with our son Gabriel, his wife Brianna and our granddaughter Chloe in November; this coincided with Chloe's first birthday. Patricia our daughter is studying in London, and – as well as seeing her there – she joined us for Christmas in Dorset. It is good to keep in touch with others by email, but here a special plea: because of very slow downloading speeds, we appreciate it if documents or photos don't exceed 50KB. An attachment came once with a single picture of around 2MB, and it took 45 minutes to download, in fits and starts. We were glad to find many Christmas cards on our return in mid-January, and suspect that others are still languishing in the sorting office in Limbe, scene of most of the postal logjams.

Before we returned to Zomba, both of us had full medical checkups at InterHealth (which is conveniently situated in the same building in London as USPG viz. Partnership House, not far from Waterloo Station). We received our booster jabs for rabies and hepatitis, and were declared no less healthy than we were before venturing to Malawi. This may be an encouragement to any of you thinking of making a visit out here, or indeed even of offering for service abroad. Many people whom we met on our parish visits wanted to know what it was like to live among such poverty, hunger and disease, and how we ourselves keep fit and well. Although in short supply, there are certainly medical services available to us. We are able to see an Indian GP in Zomba when necessary, usually on the same day when we call to make an appointment. There is also a private hospital Mwaiwathu in Blantyre which is visited by specialist consultants who fly up from Pretoria for a few days each month. The Anglican Church has its own St Luke's Hospital near our diocesan headquarters in Malosa. Bridget Le Huray, who came out with USPG at the same time as ourselves, is a nurse tutor there. As for dentists, there are several options in Blantyre, although, judging by the feedback from various friends and colleagues, their abilities vary considerably. Having begun with an Adventist dentist from South Korea, we are now much happier, if a visit is necessary, to see an Indian in private practice – possibly the best dentist we have ever known! I needed a new pair of spectacles a year ago, and (after one or two initial mistakes by a German trainee) was well served – the prescription was made up and posted out from France.

Of course, we recognise that only a small proportion of Malawians have the same access to such facilities. Without them, however, it might well happen that the contribution we can make here would be curtailed. So we regard it as important to safeguard our health. All around us, it is impossible not to notice what happens when ill-health or disease is not checked. As noted in earlier reports there are many absences from college by those attending funerals, and we hear almost daily about the further ravages of AIDS and malaria. In a remote rural setting far from any clinic no doubt things might be much worse.

One important weapon in the fight against malaria is the provision of sleeping nets, especially for children. These are expensive to buy in Britain, but can in fact be produced at a fraction of the price for wide dissemination in the Third World. With gauze over our windows as well, we find we can dispense with anti-malarial prophylactics while in Zomba, and only use them when staying at lower altitudes such as the lake shore.

Perhaps I should mention that there is no serious danger from snakes, even though we have had them in our house. My study is a previous addition to the original bungalow, and has subsided slightly because of inadequate foundations, resulting in a crack in the floor. Baby snakes have wriggled up more than once through this crack, but they are 'house snakes', excellent for keeping rats under control. Hence we are happy to live and let live. So-called 'army' ants, which march in a long column several million strong, are more of a concern, but they can easily be diverted by a sprinkling of ashes. Bats which enter in the evening via our chimney cast awesome shadows on a candlelit ceiling, but when in the morning they hang limply on the curtains we have discovered (thanks to Carolyn) how tiny they really are.

While others nevertheless face more serious setbacks and challenges on a daily basis, there is remarkable resilience and indeed much natural joy among the Malawian Africans. It remains a privilege to work here and strange to find in Britain, so much better favoured, not only grey skies but beneath them people too often grey in spirit. Words of St Paul spring to mind:

> Your abundance at the present time should supply their want, so that their abundance may supply your want, that there may be equality (2 Cor 8.14).

It is good to report that the promise of early rains has held up well, so at present it looks as if the harvest expected in April will be more adequate than in the past two years. Perversely, there is the danger of flooding in some areas. The cyclone that hit Malawi in early January had a devastating effect on the Lower Shire Valley, with many homes destroyed and entire crops wiped out. With some of the tracks impassable and several bridges brought down, it was hard for relief aid to reach the most stricken areas for several days. We are, however, glad to discover that the feeding programme at Songani is going well, although obviously there is a real struggle for many, many others.

Please pray for those who provide medical care in Malawi, especially for the staff at St Luke's Hospital, Malosa.

AN INTERREGNUM
February 2003

COLLEGE HAS GOT OFF to a good start under our new Principal, Dr Chiphangwi, who has been Vice Principal for the past two years. We have hopes that he will exercise tighter control over the finances (office supplies, for example, have been used rather extravagantly in the past), over student discipline (especially in terms of punctuality) and in implementing much needed reforms in pastoral and liturgical practice (staff decisions often fall by the wayside). One new member of staff has been recruited but I remain the only Anglican until Fr Christopher Mwawa returns in June from his further studies in the United States. As a result of staff changes, I have taken on an Old Testament course alongside two New Testament courses and ethics, together with the teaching of Anglican spirituality and practice, where this year the emphasis will be on prayer.

At St George's, now provisionally designated as the cathedral parish of the new diocese, no Malawian has yet been appointed to take charge, but the work there and in the outstations still has to be overseen. Fr Mike Gibbs, known here as a voluntary priest (in English terminology a non-stipendiary minister or NSM), has held things together in our absence for the past couple of months. We were delighted to hear at Christmas that his wife Bridget, who has had treatment for cancer over the last 15 months, is at last in the clear. The main difficulty in making any appointment for our parish for which I am now *de facto* responsible has been the absence of a resident bishop for this diocese of Upper Shire. Protests were made last year during the process of his election and confirmation, with further delays caused by a strike at Malawi's High Court from which a ruling had been sought by the dissenting faction. Once his appointment was cleared, archbishop Bernard Malango, previously in Northern Zambia, had to fulfil engagements in North America. Now that he is back, we look forward to the urgent pastoral needs of the diocese receiving proper attention as soon as he is enthroned.

His task is unenviable, given the extremely contentious dispute over his appointment. The rationale for creating an entirely new diocese resides in the need for more episcopal attention to be given to the opposite extremes of the old diocese of Southern Malawi, with the Muslim presence growing stronger around the lake shore in the north at the same time as Anglican congregations are developing in the far south. Although the division of Southern Malawi was apparently debated for some years at diocesan and provincial levels, it does not seem to have been as widely publicised and discussed within the local parishes as might have been helpful. Neither were the procedures and timetabling made as clear as might with hindsight have been desirable. It is unfortunate that the seat of opposition to bishop Bernard's translation lies with an influential and articulate group here in Zomba, who preferred a different candidate and made allegations about bishop Bernard's unsuitability. They also refused to accept the findings of an independent inquiry by an assessor from London who discounted these allegations. Having then failed to comply with the election timetable, the group petitioned the High Court to halt the election proceedings, thus dragging the internal church dispute very much into the public arena. Distorted reports reached the newspapers frequently; a dissident priest (a former journalist) studying at Chancellor College was responsible for most of these leaks, which expressed a partisan view of what was happening.

It will undoubtedly take quite a few months for normality to return to the diocese. Sadly, when I have spoken at St George's about the importance of conducting church affairs in a spirit of Christian unanimity, this has not been well received by a small minority – who make exaggerated claims to be speaking 'on behalf of others'. Consequently I have received personal abuse following my appeals for restraint. The impression I form is that, instead of showing Malawian society how it is possible to deal with disagreements in a constructive, charitable, and indeed Christian way, the church here is sadly prone to imitate the frequent unpleasant wrangling and abuse that accompanies the political life of this country. It ought to be easier for Africans to cooperate in seeking the common good, given their historical 'communitarian' spirit – whereas in reality, public affairs seem too often to reflect the rivalry between different political or religious tribes.

There are sadly similar factional strivings within the Anglican Church elsewhere. Within this province of Central Africa there is an increasingly unhappy situation in Harare, where a crony of Robert Mugabe 'serves' as bishop – and the wider church seems unwilling or unable to respond. I was told recently by another bishop that Norbert Kunongo was appointed bishop of Harare after Mugabe had bribed senior figures within the Anglican province. Kunongo's frequent brutality and intimidation against members of his diocesan flock appear just as unChristian as those employed by Zimbabwe's ruling party.

There are also unresolved issues nearer at hand in the diocese of Lake Malawi. These have arisen as a result of the disruptive influence of an American 'born again' priest. We heard him ourselves once when attending mass with a large congregation at All Saints, Nkhotakota. Much fidgeting, chatter and movement were in evidence during his sermon, which on that occasion certainly went unappreciated. We learnt subsequently that he was raised as a Baptist, and after being ordained into the Episcopal Church left it to found his own 'Church of the Living Word' as long ago as 1995. He therefore has no standing whatsoever within the Anglican Communion, and it is a mystery how he has been allowed such scope within Lake Malawi. It seems possible that he presented his Anglican credentials to bishop Peter shortly before becoming a Free Church pastor, and has kept further developments concealed from him.

Back in England there are obvious tensions remaining over issues such as women priests, and judging by the Lambeth Conference of 1998 there is a worldwide polarity between radical and conservative views on homosexual practice. Of course, these and other differences will continue to arise, and need to be resolved. My concern is that the process whereby consensus is achieved should reflect a noticeably Christian ethos.

Please pray for archbishop Bernard Malango, and for the priests and people of Upper Shire.

THE ANGLICAN HEARTLAND

March 2003

IT IS CLEAR that the bonds holding the Anglican Communion together are under severe strain. The issue dominating the headlines and tending to polarise opinion is of course about the place of homosexuals within the church's leadership. Orientation is one thing, but what some describe as deviant sexual practice is another altogether. All (or nearly all) are agreed that those whose natural inclination is towards members of their own, rather than the opposite, sex have as much a place in the church as anyone else, and should be treated with equal respect. Yet, whereas Christian teaching has for centuries with considerable scriptural backing maintained that sexual intimacy is reserved to the state of marriage, and should be open (however that is interpreted) to the fecundity of new life, the view that has emerged from the secular world is that, if one's genes predispose a person to particular forms of self-fulfilment, then to give expression to those needs and urges is their human right.

Those for whom biblical teaching and Christian practice is irrelevant will find this less of a dilemma to resolve than the churches themselves, although even they would concede that not all inborn instincts ought to be fully indulged. Most would agree that a selfish streak, a hasty temper, and a propensity towards violent behaviour, all of which may have a genetic component, should be curbed in human beings. Of all the creatures under the sun, it is surely man himself who should live up to his stature by allowing morality to govern his instincts. Certainly there is no moral objection to two men (or women) sharing a house together, whether for companionship or for financial reasons – and, if there are mutual property rights, it is perfectly fitting for these to be given appropriate legal protection.

In the debate about the morality of homosexual practice, it ought to be obvious that long-standing church tradition is well-grounded and cannot be changed in any short space of time, however much that incurs ridicule from the secular media. There is a contemporary fixation upon sexual permissiveness, which apparently relies upon a Freudian dogma that sexual repression is psychologically damaging. Those who seek to alter the church's teaching certainly need to re-examine that dogma, and in any event to allow time for thorough discussion of their views. In controversial matters it is vital for the whole body of Christians to weigh and resolve issues with as much unanimity as possible. At the present time there are probably 30,000 different Christian sects in the world, with a new one springing up somewhere almost every day. Quite a few of these are in Africa, and in Malawi itself. In many cases, they are the fruit of impatience or of personal disagreements that might eventually have been more amicably resolved. A long view of history suggests too that the preoccupations and fashions of any particular generation are often overtaken by the insights and concerns of those who come after.

Impatience would also appear to be the besetting sin of those predominantly Western Anglicans (including many Episcopalians) who regard the views of their more conservative African brothers and sisters with disdain. It should not be forgotten that numerically it is Africa which holds much the greater share of Anglican Christians today – and whose voice therefore, from a modern democratic point of view, needs to be given considerably more weight than at present it seems to be granted.

In America the number of Episcopalians is remarkably small, and the same is even more so in Scotland, compared with the huge count of Anglicans found in provinces such as Nigeria or East Africa. The total number of Anglicans worldwide is generally estimated at around 70 million, but if the BBC News website is to be believed something over one-third of these are reckoned as belonging to the Church of England. A more accurate picture would scale this contribution down to little more than 2 million, so that the Anglican Communion might be counted more modestly at just over 50 million. As three-quarters of these are in Africa, this may reasonably be described as the Anglican heartland, especially as numbers are continuing to rise there in absolute and not merely relative terms.

Truth is not wholly determined by a head count or a show of hands. African Christians point beyond their numerical superiority to their reliance not merely upon tradition but also upon reason and scriptural revelation. And within this they might well suggest the key importance for them of the human being, not as an autonomous individual standing upon his or her right to self-determination in whatever sphere, including the sexual, but as persons with mutual responsibilities.

The clearest recent exposition is to be found in Benezet Bujo's *The Ethical Dimension of Community*:

> There is a large consensus that the strengthening and the growth of life are the fundamental criteria in the realm of ethics. The members of a clan share the obligation to contribute to the growth of life of the whole community by their moral action. Usually, only that kind of behaviour which leads to the building up of the community is morally good ...
> The health (or holiness) of God's people can be seriously infringed by the actions of the individual ...
> It is important to consider that this African 'ethical community' is not restricted to the earthly community; it also includes the invisible world of the living-dead ... Within this perspective it is plain why the emphasis upon human solidarity, in both Old and New Testaments, has its appeal to the African Christian.

It hardly needs pointing out how important is the communal dimension of faith and Christian living in the New Testament. Several of Paul's comments in 1 and 2 Corinthians make this very clear, how the joys and sufferings of the individual are shared by the whole body, how his behaviour may be offensive to at least some, and how his downfall or sin is also injurious to the common good. Here too we may note Paul's self-restraint: 'Am I not free? ... Do we not have the right? ... nevertheless, we have not made use of this right, but we endure anything rather than put an obstacle in the way of the gospel of Christ' (1 Cor 9.1, 4, 12). The bishop under whom I served for over ten years in the diocese of Peterborough, Douglas Feaver, put it tersely when he explained why one has sometimes to say a pastoral No. It is, he said, 'for the sake of the others' – which was undeniably the motivation leading our Lord to his Cross. So we can fairly ask: How far in the present discussion does a same-sex 'marriage' give life and strength to the whole community? How far does it cause confusion in appearing to redefine the very word 'marriage'? How far does it mislead young people into thinking that, when they contemplate entering upon a lifelong intimate partnership, their choice between a man or a woman is quite arbitrary?

It is not as if Africans know little about homosexual practice. Recently, the BBC magazine *Focus on Africa* carried an article reporting on gay communities in South Africa. There is complementary evidence from Zomba, but of a different kind. In the vastly overcrowded prison here, many who would otherwise be considered heterosexual men have no other outlet for their sexual energy but fellow inmates – who are, alas, too often juveniles not given adequate protection by having separate cells. For most Africans this is particularly 'unnatural' in its disregard for age barriers. So while it is sometimes claimed that homosexuality is foreign to African culture, there is plenty of counter-evidence. Overwhelmingly the practice has been rejected, as disruptive of what Africans regard as divinely given norms of behaviour. Those who assume that men and women are free to choose their own norms will not appreciate this point of view, but at least within a Christian framework ought to engage more readily with it.

It appears that the spirit of Christian restraint ('for the sake of others') may at times be found more readily within mainstream African communal traditions than within the strident individualism of modern Western culture. Perhaps, it may be argued, within the close-knit life of a tribal village it was more important to maintain a common ethos than in the greater anonymity of modern urbanised societies. Yet in the Christian tradition 'the common good' has been upheld as a vital expression of the universal solidarity found in Christ. In the early centuries, following the Church's emancipation, it was Augustine of Hippo (a North African of renown!) who articulated this most clearly, asserting the primacy of God's rule above personal and privatised preferences. In one of his letters (140) he explains that this was what St Paul expected of his converts:

> The life in common of the divine and heavenly commonwealth [is one in which the faithful] 'seek not their own but the things of Jesus Christ' (cf. Phil 2.21).

Please pray for those held in Malawian prisons, especially for vulnerable young people.

PROVINCIAL AUTONOMY
April 2003

IN OUR ANGLICAN SEMINARS at college we explore aspects of Anglican history, liturgical tradition and spirituality. Inevitably the hot topic of provincial autonomy has come up for discussion recently, and what follows is a resumé of a talk given to our students.

Tensions within the Anglican Communion are nothing new. Its history is complex, and it seems that the expansion of the Anglican Church worldwide has always been fraught with legal, financial and doctrinal problems. Chiefly, the issue has been the relationship between the so-called mother church in England and the many daughter churches elsewhere in the world. Provincial autonomy is now the order of the day, but it evolved gradually under the pressure of events and needs reviewing in this twenty-first century because it is far from being a satisfactory conclusion to the problems it was supposed to answer.

It is perhaps not widely realized that for two hundred years and more after the English Reformation there were no Anglican bishops outside the British Isles. It was only after the American Declaration of Independence in 1776 that this began to change, and even then with considerable reluctance. Sixty years later there were 37 overseas bishops (27 of them in North America), but a significant increase in the middle decades of the nineteenth century more than doubled this figure. A key issue that took a century to resolve was the question of accountability: by whose authority did the rapidly growing numbers of Anglican bishops hold their position, and to whom were they answerable?

The issue came into sharp focus in the 1860s at the very time when Charles Mackenzie was making his way into the territory we now know as Malawi. Mackenzie had previously been archdeacon to the increasingly controversial figure of J. W. Colenso, bishop of Natal from 1853 to 1883. He had joined him in 1855, and had worked with him among the English settlers for several years before being appointed leader of the Universities Mission to Central Africa (UMCA) in 1860. UMCA eventually became part of my own missionary society USPG a hundred or so years later. Mackenzie was consecrated bishop for Central Africa on 1st January 1861 by bishop Gray of Cape Town. It was a novel move, much opposed (1) by low churchmen, who thought it absurd that a shepherd should be appointed without any sheep, and (2) by government ministers in England, on the grounds that he would be working outside British territory, which might give rise to unauthorised imperial expansion in 'backward and expensive' places (to quote Owen Chadwick's words).

There were both pastoral and legal issues here. While the provision of care for an anticipated missionary church made pastoral sense, what was unresolved – and whose legacy remains deeply unsatisfactory – was the latter question of 'by what authority'.

Thanks to Henry VIII the issue was not simply a question of power being centralized or dispersed. It was complicated by the fact that bishops in the Church of England have always received their appointments from the Crown; and while in some overseas dioceses the Crown's writ still ran large, in other colonies a local legislature had by now assumed many of its powers and in independent America had usurped them altogether. Yet again there were bishops such as Charles Mackenzie who found themselves beyond the bounds of anyone's protection.

Matters started to come to a head because bishop Colenso appeared to conservative theological opinion to be expressing radical views about the Bible, and in his diocese of Natal to be acting too independently. He had embarked upon a serious project to re-examine biblical interpretation from a missionary point of view – surely a laudable endeavour, given his desire to win Zulu converts to the Christian faith. However, his study of Romans led him to the conclusion that there need be no subjective response to Christ's atonement on the cross, but that henceforth it was sufficient to proclaim Christ's love as a model for all to follow. Given the contemporary controversy about *Essays and Reviews,* published one year earlier in 1860, his book was considered alarming by the English bishops, who invited Colenso to meet with some of them. He refused this offer, and turned to study the Pentateuch. He aligned himself with the latest Darwinian thinking by rejecting the early chapters of Genesis as a scientific account of creation.

Who then could bring him to account – bishop Gray of Cape Town, the archbishop of Canterbury, or the British government? There was considerable confusion about who held the reins of power in South Africa, which enabled Colenso to survive the various depositions and excommunications imposed upon him. Gray had earlier spent much time and money (some ten thousand pounds in legal fees) to ensure that the Crown gave him immediate jurisdiction over Colenso. He was sufficiently concerned about Colenso's liberal views and his published writings that he attempted to depose him. His own dean and chapter in Pietermaritzburg supported Gray's charge of heresy, and in England a gathering of bishops summoned by archbishop Longley challenged Colenso to resign. But his appointment was by letters patent from the Crown – so he appealed over bishop Gray's head, not to the archbishop of Canterbury, but to the Judicial Committee of the Privy Council. In March 1865 judgement was delivered in his favour, the court finding that in 1853 metropolitical status had not in fact been conferred upon Gray because by then Cape Colony had its own legislative assembly. Undeterred, Gray 'excommunicated' Colenso in 1866, but once again the latter's appeal was successful in retaining both his stipend from the Colonial Bishoprics Fund and his control over church property in Natal.

This unresolved duel with Gray contributed to the growing pressure (especially from Canada) for an international synod of bishops to debate Colenso's alleged heresies and to clarify the legal situation in overseas 'provinces' (as many had now come to be called). In the following year 1867 the archbishop of Canterbury did indeed invite all bishops, with the exception of Colenso, to Lambeth. It was to be, he insisted, deliberative, consultative and advisory, without aiming to pass any supposedly binding legislation. In the event, only half of those invited actually attended. Some failed to do so because of the impracticality of travel; others including the archbishop of York feared a weakening of church-state links that might be incurred if the Privy Council's ruling in Colenso's favour were to be challenged. The declaration was made that the diocese of Natal was vacant. Nevertheless, Colenso – as was his legal right – continued in office, inducing a frustrated Gray to consecrate a bishop of Maritzburg, who then shadowed Colenso. Some priests retained an allegiance to Colenso, and others transferred theirs to the new bishop. This anomalous situation continued until Colenso's death in 1883, at which point it took a further decade before the warring constituencies in Natal were more or less reconciled.

Gray's consolation lay in achieving his own independence as a 'metropolitan' (an archbishop) as a result of the Colonial Clergy Act of 1874. His canonical oath of obedience to the archbishop of Canterbury was abolished, so that henceforth Anglican provinces became effectively autonomous. Although it has now customary for the archbishop of Canterbury to invite all bishops of the Anglican Communion to a Lambeth Conference every ten years to confer together, any agreements or resolutions made there have only moral force, and are non-binding. Provincial autonomy has remained the order of the day. One of the few powers retained by the archbishop of Canterbury is the right to withhold an invitation to a Lambeth gathering.

In my ten years on General Synod in England I can scarcely recall anyone intervening in a debate to ask how decisions and recommendations might be seen from afar. It invariably appeared that the Church of England was intent upon pursuing its own autonomous (i.e. independent) course; any sense of being at least partially accountable to other provinces was non-existent. Consequently, the Anglican Communion now finds itself adopting mutually incompatible teachings and policies in different provinces. Whatever solution is proposed – such as the unlikely elevation of the archbishop of Canterbury to a quasi-papal position of authority, or a supposedly binding form of global consultation – the one stumbling block will inevitably be the establishment of the Church of England. So long as it is in the last resort legally beholden to Parliament, there will be a parliamentary fly in every ointment; where major changes are in view, even if synodical procedures within different provinces could be suitably reconciled, agreement across the Anglican Communion might conceivably be challenged within the British parliament. The ghost of Henry VIII is still at large. How absurd that the *de facto* leader of a world-wide church is appointed by the former imperial power's Prime Minister, who need not even be a Christian, let alone an Anglican.

Please pray for the disestablishment of the Church of England.

POWER CRISIS
May 2003

AT THE TIME OF WRITING, harvesting is beginning to take place. The returns are better than last year but the prospects for the many who were unable to afford fertiliser are none too rosy. There were earlier fears that the record rainfall in February and March would destroy much of the maize. Electrical storms, usually in the late afternoon or evening, were an almost daily occurrence and several people near Zomba were killed by lightning. Fortunately, April was much drier.

The heavy rains also significantly raised the level of water in Lake Malawi, which flooded along its outflow, the river Shire (pronounced Shee-ray). This then washed away much vegetation, which got sucked into the hydroelectric turbines further down the river, making power cuts inevitable. But there was worse to come: at the beginning of March, the largest power station of all was completely flooded when a rusted iron flange gave way on one of the bypass pipes. This need not have happened if regular maintenance had been carried out on these flanges. All of the turbines are out of commission waiting their turn to be thoroughly dried and cleaned, a process which is likely to take several months (so we are informed). Frequent power cuts are therefore anticipated for the foreseeable future, since this second power station supplies roughly half of all electricity consumption in the country. One of the national newspapers suggested it was time for Malawi to have a nuclear power station, on the grounds that less maintenance might be needed!

Since then, more evenings than not have been spent by lamp-light, and our emergency gas ring is being well used. A restoration to something like normal services is promised within the next few months. Emailing, and other office work, is only possible during a morning or an afternoon – but not both on the same day, and perhaps only on alternate days! Bulletins are sometimes issued as to when cuts may be expected, but they are not wholly reliable. Of course, we're fortunate to have electricity at all, given that ninety-five per cent of Malawian homes are not yet connected to a supply. We smile ruefully whenever there are statements in the Western media pronouncing that soon everyone, including schools and colleges, will be on the internet. The reality is that perhaps some three per cent of the world's population has present access, with the figure edging slowly upwards.

There is good news to report about Carolyn. She is becoming increasingly competent in her chosen career, and has held a temporary office job since the middle of February. We are hoping that this, or something equivalent, will become a permanent position, as she enjoys it so much and is continuing to learn new skills. We are also waiting to hear if she has been successful in her bid to become a trainee with the Malawi Revenue Authority. There were 300 applicants in all but there were many places to be filled because of the considerable loss of existing staff due to AIDS and other illnesses. The civil service, the army, the police, the teaching and health professions are all affected in the same way. It is almost impossible for enough recruits to be found to match the many who have died.

At Songani, the demands continue to increase. The number of orphans registered in the group of villages has climbed this year from 410 to 450. The feeding programme during the hunger months was successful and the project continues to expand in various ways. For example, cowsheds, built by the villagers with help from the carpentry group, are now nearly ready to accommodate the five cows that have been bought to supply the children with milk. Soap began to be produced in January and is selling well. Earlier this year, we ran into difficulties when many of the skills training sessions for the older children had to be cancelled due to the heavy rains. At present, there is no alternative to teaching carpentry, metalwork, bricklaying, tailoring (and so on) out in the open air. We hope that a simple shelter will have been constructed before the next wet season.

Elsewhere, the relief feeding operations, managed mainly by non-governmental organisations in the different districts, have worked better than initially seemed likely. Deaths by starvation have been fewer than last year; but pockets of hunger remain, and, in some places (as in Zimbabwe), the food distribution has been politicised – with ruling party members getting the lion's share.

In our own garden, the rains have kept plants flourishing. A couple of acacia trees that were planted only three years ago are currently in full yellow blossom. Our many poinsettias, which grow vastly bigger than the potted versions seen in England around Christmas, turn red at this time and will stay red until much later in the year. Avocado pears have been plentiful, and it remains a good season for bananas and paw-paws, all of which help to provide us with a daily fruit salad. Recently the paw paw tree, of which the trunk consists of pulp rather than wood, keeled across the telephone line, putting it out of action. It was actually mended just half an hour later – but then, the telephone exchange is only half a mile away, at the other end of our road. Further away, we might not have been nearly so fortunate.

Inside the house, there have been several plumbing emergencies, but we're content so long as our cold water supply remains intact. With unreliable plumbing standards, there is a distinct risk of leaks following any plumbing repair. Since we pay for our water, which is metered, we keep to what is essential. If we need hot water, we simply boil the kettle.

On the Anglican development site, with our gardener Kidman's help and advice from our good friend John Wilson, we have been busy planting out hundreds of cuttings from our own plants and shrubs. In this climate, they take very readily. We have seen a green lawn starting to flourish only a few weeks after transplanting the grass (root by root!). So the LKTC environment is already beginning to take shape. Several ordinands have been living with their families here for the past year.

One of Sarah's sisters and her husband will be with us shortly for a fortnight's stay. We're greatly looking forward to their visit, as it gives us an opportunity to get out and about a little bit more ourselves. It will be their first taste of Africa.

Once again we express our thanks for letters and prayers received. Incoming mail is generally good at the moment but outgoing mail seems to be subject to theft, as well as to considerable delays. News about life in England and about the church there is always very welcome, as little else apart from war is heard on the BBC World Service just at present.

Please pray for those who maintain the essential services in Malawi.

OUR NEW BISHOP
June 2003

THE KEY EVENT in recent months was undoubtedly the enthronement of archbishop Bernard Malango as bishop of our new Anglican diocese of Upper Shire, attended by representatives of all the dioceses in Malawi, provincial visitors and Vice-President Malewezi, who is an Anglican.

If rain is a propitious sign in Africa, we were certainly well blessed, although the thunder and the constant drumming on the church roof rendered some of the service inaudible to those seated further back. Among the many welcoming speeches, I duly delivered greetings from bishop Mano Rumalshah, Director of USPG.

In his charge, the archbishop particularly highlighted the need to evangelise in the rural areas, reminding the clergy it was a privilege to be called to serve there, even if the urban centres with their better schools and amenities often have a more attractive appeal.

Following the archbishop's installation, new appointments in the diocese were made and several confirmation services took place, generally with high numbers of candidates. Near us at St Mary's, Chinamwali, for example, there were 162. That figure may startle readers back in England, but a year or so ago I learnt of comparable numbers from our neighbouring parish in the Blantyre direction. In two years the priest there had built four new churches, and his parishioners had moulded and burnt sufficient bricks to start constructing a new school near the main church. In the same period there were 1321 baptisms spread over the 20 congregations in his care, and 334 candidates had been presented for confirmation. During a Sunday morning visit I helped to enrol many new members of the Mothers Union and to licence several new lay readers. Mine was the only vehicle outside the church – everyone else had either walked or (to my surprise) had cycled. I counted nearly eighty bicycles stacked up outside. The truck did, however, prove its worth and earn its keep, as we ferried over a number of concrete window grids for the rectory.

I am glad to report that at last St George's, Zomba, has a new priest, a warm and seemingly energetic man with five delightful children. His wife teaches at the prison school, and he also serves as archdeacon. He needs our prayers as he struggles to unify the parish and to consolidate its finances. Before the archdeacon moved in, archbishop Bernard answered my urgent call to come over from Malosa to minister the last rites to the ailing church member (mentioned previously) who had opposed his appointment. There was a moving reconciliation just before he died, which I hope will influence some of those who still seem intransigently opposed to the bishop. Sarah and I are now free to travel further afield on Sundays to support other clergy, particularly as the dry season makes the tracks more negotiable.

On Easter Sunday, I celebrated and preached at the inauguration of a new congregation in the parish of Magomero. During the mass four babies, two little girls and two young men were baptised. The service took place in a well-scented barn on a tobacco estate. The parish choir joined us, along with girls from St Agnes' Guild and representatives of the Mother's Union. Perhaps the most exuberant part of this joyful occasion was the offering of gifts. There were the usual speeches that concluded our morning which lasted four hours in all. We learnt that this was the eighth new congregation to be established in Fr Brighton Malasa's first year as parish priest – by any account, quite an achievement.

Back in Zomba, the teaching programme has gone well over the past term. The college draws a few students from outside Malawi, and one new student from Zimbabwe had the greatest difficulty in obtaining a visa to join us, but did so eventually ten weeks after the start of term. We hosted a staff party early on in the year and also entertained visitors from elsewhere. The bishop-elect of Niassa, whose huge diocese in Mozambique borders the parish of St George across Lake Chilwa, called with his family *en route* for Blantyre, their nearest sizeable town despite being in a different country. Soon afterwards, the college received a group of students from a Mozambican seminary in the opposite direction, to the west of the Kirk Mountains. Their leader, a descendant of the great Paul Kruger, stayed with us and explained (among other things) that the timber on the roof of his vehicle was not, as we had supposed, firewood for camping, but a portable bridge often called into play when crossing the many streams in their remote terrain. This visit was part of the networking that now takes place between several theological colleges in Southern Africa. The scheme is spearheaded by the University of Stellenbosch, whose priorities are to increase HIV/AIDS awareness, and to equip future clergy better for the training of lay people.

Now we look forward to one of our regular visits from Fr Rodney Hunter, a long-serving USPG missionary In Malawi. When we arrived here he was looking after a far-flung rural parish, but after treatment for cancer in England he has returned to live within easy reach of the hospital in Nkhotakota. He seems to be as active as ever in the parish of All Saints. We value any opportunity that allows us to meet other Anglican clergy in Malawi, and are particularly pleased to have heard that the Rt Revd Jackson Biggers, retired bishop of Northern Malawi, will be taking up residence on Zomba plateau for several months each year, with the aim of assisting in this diocese of Upper Shire. He has charged me with the task of getting a phone line in order before his arrival! I hope to achieve this before being out of action for some minor surgery in Blantyre.

Please pray for newly established congregations within the diocese of Upper Shire, and for those recently baptised or confirmed.

Mulanje from our garden

THE PROCESS OF FORMATION
July 2003

STUDENTS ENTERING COLLEGE often come from relatively limited and under-resourced schooling, making their first year with us something of a struggle as they adjust to different methods of study and indeed different expectations. They may, for example, have been used to absorbing quantities of information, which is then reproduced as fully and as accurately in examinations. Independent reading and reflection may well have been largely absent from the learning process.

So it is always rewarding for staff to be able to look back over three or four years to see how each final year ordinand has progressed, both academically and spiritually, during their time with us. And while classroom teaching and discussion is important to cover much of the ground relevant to their formation, there are other times, perhaps in smaller groups, that can be very fruitful. Our Wednesday afternoon pastoral sessions involve students from different year groups, from different sending churches, and from different parts of the country. Again, our weekly Anglican seminars enable us to explore more of our own tradition, and the termly weekend retreats with Anglican year groups open up many wider issues.

Here are some of the concerns voiced by our third year Anglicans during a recent weekend away together:-

- For all their pride in belonging to an independent country, they are aware that many of the hopes and dreams at the time of Malawi's inauguration are far from having been realised – and that throughout Africa these are frustrated by tribal and ethnic divisions which can lead to thousands or millions being displaced from their homes, by corruption in high places that does nothing to narrow the enormous gap between rich and poor, and by endless crises of poverty and hunger.
- They are ashamed that there are beggars on the streets, that often not even water is available in government hospitals, that HIV/AIDS remains so rampant, that many locations have minimal educational resources with teachers and nurses sometimes going unpaid for

months at a time. Yet they see government ministers being driven in top-of-the-range Mercedes limousines and the President himself having five state residences costing £2 million a year to maintain.

- They were shocked by statistics released last year relating to the main Malawian school certificate. 28000 students sat these examinations, but only 8000 gained the full certificate – and 6000 (presumably many of whom belonged to church congregations or schools) were failed for cheating. Corruption, they concluded, is not only a problem at the top.
- They express sadness too that the brain-drain of those who do gain good qualifications still continues to empty Malawi of much needed professionals. Roughly one-third of all newly qualified nurses end up working in Britain for the National Health Service, while wards in their own country remain closed for lack of staff. Where, they wondered, is the Christian commitment to look after those in greatest need?
- They know that Malawi still relies financially to a great extent upon sales of tobacco, which is harmful. There is some anger that this was first planted on a substantial scale by British colonialists for their own prosperity. Yet why, they wonder, has no alternative crop taken its place – and why, when it is food that people really need, is not that grown instead?
- They ask why, if Western countries are anxious for fighting to cease in the world, in particular within Africa itself, do they seem so keen to export weapons and combat aircraft? Do they not appreciate how rapidly they can fall into the wrong hands, and that in Zimbabwe the aircraft supplied recently 'for training purposes only' will bomb innocent people?
- They have been alarmed by the recent spate of violence occasioned by the summary deportation of suspected Al Qaeda terrorists at the bidding of America. Following a minimal or non-existent legal process here, there has been a series of attacks by Muslims on Christian churches and on NGO offices, particularly around the southern lakeshore. Previous relations between the different faith communities have been remarkably harmonious, so our ordinands

are anxious about the readiness to identify Christianity with Western political interests.
- Although they realise that Christianity is apparently a success story in Malawi, with new churches constantly being built, and on Sundays impressive streams of churchgoers heading along the roads towards them, they suspect that underneath this outward show Christian faith can be much shakier. In times of crisis, they tell me, people are prone to turn elsewhere, seeking more 'powerful' remedies which for many are still found in traditional beliefs. Some years ago a torrential storm in Zomba brought a massive rock-and-mud slide down the mountain: the village most affected then offered animal sacrifices to Napolo, the god who rules from the mountain heights. The people of that village remain staunch Presbyterians to this day, but they might well have been Anglicans or Catholics.

After our discussions, I think they understand that it is as much their challenge as it is mine (and ours) to begin to find some of the answers. My role as a missionary from a different culture is not necessarily to suggest the way forward, but rather to guide students to discover the right questions. Across the world, we need each other as partners to discern what the Spirit is saying to the churches.

By the time they graduate from college, each student is required to have focused on an issue of topical concern, and to have presented a dissertation, not only on paper, but also in an open seminar attended by staff and other students. We have just concluded a series of well-considered presentations concerned with, for example, the discipline and guidance of church members, Eucharistic worship up and down the country, and the use of tribal languages in relation to church growth. My own particular contribution was to invite discussion of a recent sermon in which I attempted (helpfully or not?) to inculturate the gospel message:

When God made the world he planted mango trees everywhere. All year round, wherever you went – even if far from home – there were ripe mangoes waiting to be picked. But as time went on, there were more and more humans, and not enough mangoes: so some people went mango raiding. They would strip trees in other villages, and leave nothing for the local people or for those passing by. So there were bad feelings and much fighting, and God said, 'Enough of this! There shall be a law of mangoes. I now decree that you may only pick mangoes that grow within a thousand paces of your home.'

This law was a good thing, because it tried to restore peace and bring order. But it also tempted people to go out at night and steal fruit without being seen – so there was less fighting but more suspicion, and hardship for those who kept the law. So what was God to do? He thought of making an extra law, forbidding people to travel more than a thousand paces from their homes. But he realised that with more restrictions there would only be more lawlessness. Maybe instead he should blight all the mango trees, which would certainly prevent any fruit being stolen? Yet again he thought, the people would starve, and find no joy in life, so he stayed his hand.

Instead, he hatched a less obvious plan. His son, whose name was Joshua in Hebrew, went to live quietly in a village for thirty years, never going very far and never stealing anything himself, although he certainly knew mango raiders came and went all the time, causing anger and mayhem. Then an idea came to him. He suggested to his friends that, in their several villages, they should each keep a stock of mangoes ready in baskets for any outsiders to help themselves. They thought this was quite crazy, but they tried it. At first it seemed to work: the raids died down. But then, greed got the upper hand: 'We've only to kill whoever it is puts these mangoes out, and the rest will be ours for good.'

Word of this plot spread quickly, and Joshua's friends went into hiding. Not so Joshua himself: 'Take my mangoes, take me too,' he said. Thus his fate was sealed, and things seemed just as bad as ever. Yet to their astonishment, Joshua reappeared dramatically in the very place where his friends were hiding. 'When we gave the mangoes away, did you go hungry? When you lost me, did you think that was the end? You must have faith – and courage to go on giving and sharing.' So they emerged from hiding, and went out to share whatever they had, mangoes and all, whatever it cost to bring peace to God's world.

Whether helpful or not, the exercise provoked a lively debate!

Please pray for wisdom in the coming generation of church leader to guide their people aright and to promote the values of God's kingdom within Malawi.

A BEAUTIFUL COUNTRY
August 2003

DURING OUR FOUR YEARS in Malawi, we have regularly seen life in the villages around Zomba and have visited a number of St George's outstations (which can sometimes take nearly two hours on unmade tracks), as well as parishes further afield. There have also been breaks when we've been able to explore some of the wonderful scenery elsewhere.

Malawi boasts hills and mountains, tropical forest, savannah, riverine marshes and (its jewel) Lake Malawi itself. Even without leaving home we have enjoyed the wonder and beauty of our own garden which has attracted monkeys and a whole variety of birds, such as louries, woodpeckers, sunbirds, bulbuls and owls. Just one hour's drive away is Liwonde National Park, bordering the Shire river, which is where we have usually tried to take family members visiting from England. There we can rely upon seeing bird life in abundance, and always antelopes, kudu, warthogs, hippos, crocodiles and elephants.

In the southern end of the park I was once on my own with an unarmed guide walking through the bush. The previous week there had been lions around, but he believed they'd moved east into the hills. After a couple of hours, after emerging from the woods we approached a shrub-covered mound: 'Now that,' he explained, 'is exactly the sort of place where young lions lie in wait for their prey.' As it happened, none was on duty at the time. One week later, this over-confident guide met with disaster. He was tracking elephants with a party of English visitors, but approached the herd too closely. Since there were baby elephants to be protected, a bull elephant turned to attack. All the guide could do was to pull his tail, which failed to free the woman (a nurse) he had already seized with his trunk. She was thrown to the ground and trampled to death. Despite this, the guide's licence was neither suspended nor revoked.

At other times, the authorities did display a concern for public safety. When, in our first year, we took a trip on the old (1950s) passenger tub MV Ilala, which each week sails northwards from Monkey Bay taking local people and essential supplies to the lakeshore villages, our departure was delayed by several hours until the government safety inspector was satisfied that various repairs had been properly carried out. One week after we'd disembarked, a terrible accident occurred in the night. The two ship's boats were ferrying people ashore at Chipoka when a violent storm blew up and capsized one of them. Only the men aboard were able to swim, so a score or more of women and children drowned. Our feeling was that, as these boats were (from our own observation) invariably overladen, there may have been even thirty or forty who died. At the inquiry the captain insisted that there were precisely twenty-two deaths, which also happened to be the very number that each of the ship's boats was licensed to carry. The truth will presumably never be known.

The only dangers encountered on the Malawi mainland were manmade. As we travelled once towards the western escarpment at Dzalanyama we found the tracks increasingly waterlogged, and finally ground to a halt in the mud. Although we appeared to be in the middle of nowhere, we were soon surrounded by a crowd, including many children, who enjoyed pushing us out. They were duly rewarded! A worse experience happened on Nyika plateau when heading for one of main viewpoints. Suddenly we found the grasslands around us catching fire, with us trapped in the middle. It happened to be the time of year when this was deliberately induced, but no warning had been issued to visitors. The only way to escape was to drive straight forwards down the track, which had a thinner covering of grass and fewer flames than elsewhere. I trusted to luck that our fuel tank would be spared, and we made it to safety.

It was also a truck ride that was to give us a few unplanned thrills down south. Our house, on the slopes of Zomba mountain, faces south and on a clear day presents us with a lovely vista of the Mulanje range forty miles away in the distance. Here are the highest mountains between Kilimanjaro and the Drakensbergs, stretching a good thirty miles across. We have made three trips into them, each time staying in the mountain huts provided. A climb of three thousand feet up to the plateau is necessary from any of the valleys below, but since the local economy relies on visitors hiring local youths as porters it's easy to offload the burden of all one's kit. Our first porter was named Hanky – most confusing whenever he was addressed by name! His ambition was to read computer studies at college.

He was tall and fast, and quite unconcerned when the straps of our Chinese-made rucksack, bought the day before in Zomba market, collapsed. He simply balanced it on his head as he continued to skip along in the fastest hike we'd ever experienced. When, on our descent, I inquired how long it might take to reach a stream flowing down below, he said 'It would take me twenty minutes, but as we're going so slowly it may well be more like forty.' We discovered later that there was an annual porters' race, in which they went up the mountain side, around and down, to cover in a few hours a route that took us three days. One year the winner went on, with no training other than his experience as a porter, to compete in his first marathon in Lilongwe. He won, in a time of two hours fifteen minutes.

For our longest hike in Mulanje, which was a traverse of the whole range, we took two porters, as of course there had to be sufficient food plus any necessary cooking utensils to last several days. The weather was perfect, and we successfully made it before descending to the village well east of our starting point. It was by then about the middle of the day, and with no organised public transport we needed to find a truck heading back west. I inquired in a shop, where they pointed out a driver waiting to load up passengers. He needed, he said, a dozen to make his trip worthwhile, so thought he might be setting off in an hour or two. I offered him extra for our fares if he went slightly sooner, and a deal was struck. I was perched in the open back, which proved to be a better place than in the one passenger seat offered to Sarah sat, who thereby became far more conscious of the vehicle's deficiencies, starting with an entire absence of springs in her seat and a crazed windscreen. Our nerves were tested most of all as we approached the narrow plank bridges over the various streams. The driver invariably halted first, because his radiator leaked and he needed to top up with water. But we had become aware that his steering was also defective, and we seldom advanced consistently in a straight line. On a section of ordinary track, with hardly any other traffic around, this was not a problem, whereas crossing an unprotected narrow bridge did raise certain doubts. On this occasion we were lucky and made it safely back to base.

We have just returned from a ten day break, during which I was able to convalesce after two hernia operations in Blantyre. Three years after our first trip on the *Ilala*, we sailed with her across the lake to stay in

Mozambique, in a remote corner that (as we came to discover later on) still bears the devastating marks of the civil war. The small port of Cobue where we disembarked remains half in ruins, with many walls pock-marked with bullet holes. A large Catholic seminary was devastated, and the main church burnt down, in the fighting. People only began to trickle back to this remote corner less than ten years ago. The lodge where we stayed helps to provide its neighbours with solar power and other resources.

Since vehicular access over rough tracks is still very difficult, most supplies are brought in by boat, such as the Ilala. Before we reached land we saw one of the most astonishing sights of the lake. From a distance it looked like clouds of smoke, but as we drew nearer it proved to be columns of mating flies rising up perhaps two hundred feet or more above the water. The centre of each column, so we were told, was where the males clustered together, viewed by females on the periphery who were talent spotting, their ideal partner being as symmetrically-shaped as possible.

Our first night ashore was quite magical. A ketch met the Ilala and we sailed southwards by moonlight for about ninety minutes until landing on a wooden jetty decked with an array of paraffin lanterns. These also illuminated the midnight feast that followed. The next morning we woke to a cloudless sky and discovered the clean white sands after which the place is named – *nkwichi*, meaning 'squeaky'. Little did we know then, as we saw for ourselves a few days later, that crocodiles flourished in the water only half a mile along the shore. Fortunately crocodiles are essentially lazy, and prefer to keep an eye on places that are more frequented by human beings. Hippos, we'd already learnt, can be less predictable. Over on the opposite side of the lake we'd once seen half of a dugout canoe abandoned on the beach. A local boy told us then: 'My father was out fishing in his dugout, when hippos swam past, and one of them attacked, biting the boat in half and killing my father at the same time.'

On the Sunday during our stay, we were taken by ketch a couple of miles up the coast to the small thatched Anglican church of St Martin, Mala. Although most villagers had fled across the lake into Malawi for refuge, a few had returned here with their children. As they spoke Chichewa, we were able to celebrate mass together. Seldom did they ever receive a visit from a priest, so it was a joy to be there, following in the revered footsteps of William Percival Johnson a hundred years earlier. As we pushed off from the water's edge, they all crowded down on the beach I was given a keepsake which I shall treasure: a little broom made from slender reeds on the shore. The following day it was agreed that several of the men from the congregation would walk across to our camp to discuss outstanding issues and future plans. It was clear when we met that further training, to help them lead Christian life and worship at St Martin's in the absence of a priest, was top of their agenda. One of them actually expressed interest in ordination, and wanted advice about the necessary steps to be taken.

Now we're here at college again for our final term. We are helping Carolyn prepare to move back to her village which is just outside Zomba. She is having her own small house built, adjacent to those of her remaining family. As she has a steady income from her secretarial employment, she will be the main support for several younger cousins. We went together to buy the necessary roofing sheets in town, and rapidly found that, to prevent them trailing on the ground behind the truck, Carolyn needed to sit on top of them the whole way there, which made quite a spectacle! Once the house is finished we are confident that she will be well set up.

We've also supplied Kidman, who is still assisting with the many cuttings for the LKTC site, with much needed items for his eldest daughter Eleza. She is a very sick HIV positive woman with TB and shingles, who has little energy for life. She has recently been in hospital, where for much of the time she had to share a bed with another patient. She has come home with medication, and we have made her more comfortable by getting a foam mattress for her, complete with a blanket and pillow, and a change of clothes. Previously she had only a mat to sleep on, with a few sacks to give her any warmth. She feels happier now, but the prospects are not good.

Looking ahead, we're pleased that our successors in this house have gladly agreed to take care of Lily, our Rhodesian ridgeback bitch. And the *Why Wait?* project that is proving so effective in promoting Christian teaching about personal relationships is acquiring our truck to further their work throughout secondary schools up and down the country.

Please pray for isolated Christian communities who maintain their faith with little outside support.

NTIYA NEWS

September 2003

THE VILLAGE OF NTIYA has not previously been mentioned in these reports, an omission I must now remedy. It is situated on the opposite side of Zomba to Songani, to the west of the army barracks. It is however probably closer to the hospital than we are ourselves, which is very important for some of the young women there. Living not far from army personnel, they are constantly under threat of sexual exploitation. Hence there is a high incidence of HIV/AIDS among them, and – as at Songani – many children in the area are already orphaned.

Sarah came to know of this village and its neighbours last year through Ethel, whose husband Fr Howard has been away studying, but prior to that had been rector of St George's. Her mother Amayi Mpesi lives in Ntiya, and as a devout Catholic has made the care of AIDS sufferers, their offspring and their orphans, very much her personal responsibility. She is officially designated by the local authority as one of their AIDS coordinators, and has attended a number of training courses. She has taken Sarah to see some of her people in their homes (often little more than shelters). Rose, for example, is a young mother with four children. She is HIV positive, and is in and out of hospital all the time, diagnosed as seriously ill with TB. In fact, her condition seems to be terminal. When this was discovered, her husband simply abandoned her and disappeared, so the children are now largely in the care of her own mother who looks after six others as well.

By contrast, Clement and Gloria are two teenage sibling orphans with no one left in their family at all to help them. They live in a small outhouse next to the decaying huts where they were brought up. These once constituted a homestead for their grandparents and extended family, but in Malawi some still follow the tradition not to live in the house of any deceased person. Fortunately for them Amayi Mpesi has agreed to be their guardian, and is able to provide extra maize and some clothing. It is sad that Gloria is herself dying of AIDS. The illness started only a few months ago, but already she is frail and sickly, and life for her is now a constant day-to-day struggle.

Amayi Mpesi also helps in the provision of nursery care for five mornings each week. Recently two young English visitors to Zomba who stayed with a friend – a regular worshipper at St George's – have provided extra funds for her work. This has enabled her to get a thatched shelter built for the nursery, and to buy extra food for them. She then experienced a very frustrating disappointment. When two truckloads of relief aid arrived in Ntiya, only members of Muluzi's own political party were allowed to attend the distribution of maize – so these children missed out. Another disappointment is that, despite several new bore holes having been dug just four years ago for the provision of clean water, three of them are already out of use. Sarah has, however, been able to take over bundles of second-hand clothes for the children, purchased in one or more of the many village markets. Amayi Mpesa is always very appreciative, and is punctilious in writing thank-you notes beginning 'My dear daughter in Christ'. She provides details of how every kwacha she has received has been spent.

I am relieved to report that several others of the expatriate community here in Zomba are taking an active interest both in Ntiya and in Songani, so that when we leave at the end of next month it should be possible for both projects to gain the support they need. After a gap of several years Songani is likely to obtain a further grant from War on Want, and will have experienced advice in helping with the necessary paperwork. As with Ntiya, so in Songani Mr Mpaya is meticulous in keeping his account. Even if there is often room for doubt about various departments of government, we feel very confident in his honesty and reliability.

A lecturer at Chancellor College has also agreed to provide funding for ten orphaned teenagers from SCCG to attend secondary school. At the same time she is employing Mr Kuswele's carpentry group to construct a fence around her garden. Although the soap-making project has been going well on Saturday mornings since the beginning of the year, and has found a ready market for sales, there has been a problem in the supply line since last month. Silcom silicate is apparently an essential ingredient used for hardening the soap into blocks, but it seems that a new supply will now need to be sourced. The milk project is thriving, and one of the cows has produced two calves. Milk that is in excess of local requirements (for the youngest orphans themselves) is sold off. The government agency that helped to fund the project is suitably impressed, and has agreed to provide a grant for the much anticipated maize mill.

And much nearer home, Carolyn's plans are gathering pace. We have helped her to obtain all the necessary building materials, and will be giving her most of our kitchen goods when we leave so that it will be adequately furnished. While it is being built, she will stay next door with her remaining aunt. She is now working with one of our Dutch colleagues at ZTC who is compiling a new Chichewa-English dictionary. We think that the lecturer and his family from Northern Ireland who will be moving into our house will also be glad to give work to the people we have used in the garden and for keeping watch at night.

I thought I would conclude with a couple of crime stories that have been in the news of late, each with a somewhat unexpected twist:

- Zomba's prison is located not so far from Ntiya, where a local resident was sentenced to a term of imprisonment. What was his crime? He had been discovered making frequent visits *into* the prison grounds at night. He crawled easily under the perimeter fence, thence made his way to the shed where tools such as hoes and spades were kept for the prisoners' daily work schedule. He managed to steal several, one at a time. Presumably the magistrate was confident that he wouldn't go home too often?
- Elsewhere, a policeman was sentenced to 3 years imprisonment for the theft of a relatively small amount of cash – equivalent to some fifty pounds. At much the same time, one diocese here found that an archdeacon had been siphoning off thousands of pounds from church funds, but decided not to charge him for the offence. Instead he was punished by being removed from his urban parish and sent to serve in a rural location!

Please pray for Amayi Mpesi, for Kennedy Mpoya, for the many people they help – and for all the colleagues, students and friends we shall leave behind in Zomba.

LINKS AND PLANS
October 2003

FOR MOST OF OUR TIME in Zomba, I have been the only Anglican member of staff in this ecumenical college. The Anglican Church in Malawi, unlike the Presbyterian and Catholic Churches here, has been slow to equip its own clergy with further studies, enabling them to be theological trainers.

So we rejoice that Fr Christopher Mwawa has now returned from studies abroad with a Master's degree. Two other priests are completing doctoral programmes this year, and at least three others are pursuing Master's degrees. This bodes well for the future, holding out the possibility that the number of Anglican ordinands in training may be able to expand. At present, financial, housing and staffing constraints limit us to about eight recruits each year - that is two from each of the four dioceses. Yet many more than this offer themselves for the sacred ministry.

With growing numbers of congregations, the need for more clergy increases from year to year. The parish of St George's, Zomba may serve to illustrate the point. Last year, one of its large congregations (St Mary's, Chinamwali) became a separate parish with its own priest, a dedicated young man recently from ZTC. Nearly 30 congregations over perhaps one hundred square miles still remain with St George's, served by two full time Malawian priests and given extra help on Sundays by one or two of us based in Zomba. In the diocese of Northern Malawi there are currently five parishes, each with many outstations, unmanned through shortage of clergy.

Having an experienced (and well-travelled) primate in archbishop Bernard, it now seems possible that his North American contacts may bring a little assistance. In June, we received visitors from the diocese of Quincy, and there is talk of several priests coming successively to Zomba for one year each. Seeing the needs here for themselves appears to have confirmed their commitment to missionary service. (They seemed particularly pleased that LKTC has flush toilets, which they were able to test out, even if they were rather shocked to learn of my impending treatment in a local hospital where hygienic standards might not match those in the States.)

A similar visit in August from the diocese of Birmingham and its new Ugandan bishop, the Rt Revd John Sentamu, has also brought life to an existing link. Sarah and I met bishop John at Malosa at the archbishop's house. Despite being familiar with his native continent, bishop John spoke of his shock at the degree of poverty in Malawi, which was far worse than anything he had previously experienced. In his home country of Uganda, he said, the climate is favourable and the soil is bountiful, enabling different crops to be grown throughout the year. But Malawi, he realised, is wholly dependent upon adequate rainfall in just three months of the year. Even then, the greater density of population means that the harvest will be insufficient without the use of fertiliser, which is seldom affordable.

Bishop John spoke also of being deeply moved by his visit to the lakeshore at Nkhotakota where, in the graveyard of All Saints' Church, are the burial places of many of the earliest English missionaries. The crosses erected for them carry eloquent testimony to the sacrificial devotion of those young men one hundred years ago. Most of them died under the age of thirty, after only two or three years of missionary service. And yet, the bishop observed, others came willingly to replace them.

So we are left wondering, Who will follow us? It is our hope that the plans now well laid for LKTC to begin its independent existence will mature by 2005. This will enable the Anglican Church in Malawi to be more self-reliant. Yet even so, it is good for wider partnerships to continue, and for exchanges of personnel to take place from time to time. Archbishop Bernard has already asked me if I would facilitate such support from the UK by being his Commissary there. On his recent visit to St George's he graciously installed my colleague Mike Gibbs (a farm manager who is also a voluntary priest) and myself as canons of the diocese.

At the outset of our stay in Zomba it was clear that LKTC represented the shape of things to come. We are glad to have played our part in facilitating this, and will hope to raise awareness of its needs in the future. Consideration has already been given in an outline draft to its financial needs and its funding. At this stage, it is reckoned that the costs would be shared as follows: 50% of necessary income should be forthcoming from the four dioceses, in equal shares; 25% is likely to be available from the Anglican Council of Malawi; the final 25% will depend upon donations and any income-generating schemes that can be developed. I hope it is fully appreciated that, with diocesan funds being very stretched already, LKTC will certainly suffer if the new Christian College in Lilongwe starts to compete for financial support. A potentially divisive reference to the provision of training for ordination has already reappeared in its stated objectives. This may just be an allusion to possible non-residential pre-ordination courses, although I suspect otherwise. The question inevitably arises, Are the Malawian bishops all equally committed to LKTC?

News from other African dioceses suggests that income-generating schemes are steadily becoming a familiar part of the fund-raising scene. Further south in Lesotho and Swaziland investments have been made in shopping and / or business centres. Already here at St Peter's Seminary In Zomba students are engaged in a number of different food-producing projects, such as chicken rearing and fruit growing, which will not only save money on shopping bills but hopefully produce a surplus for cash sales. The construction of fish pools is on their future agenda. For LKTC there has been discussion of constructing hostel accommodation in the town to rent out to university students. Obviously such schemes require capital outlay, which is not necessarily readily available: but once in place some flow of income can be expected independent of donor aid.

In terms of an annual budget for LKTC, it is clear that provision will need to be made for principal items such as staff salaries and pensions, student living costs, office requirements (including examination fees), building improvements and repairs, vehicle and travel expenses, utility bills and rates. Hopefully there will be money to improve library stock and facilities on a regular basis. In Malawi sums need to be available too for contingencies such as medical and funeral expenses. Our experience from ZTC suggests that cash flows, especially from the dioceses, may be somewhat erratic, so budgets will need a degree of flexibility.

A major new project such as LKTC takes more time to plan here in Africa than perhaps it might on other continents. Much depends on economic circumstances, as well as on the health and capability of the people most involved. In turn, climatic conditions (i.e. weather patterns) loom larger in the state of the economy in Malawi than they do in the UK, and the future impact of AIDS is at this stage hard to predict. Forward planning, as opposed to hand-to-mouth existence, is in any case a relatively unfamiliar exercise. Nor is it easy for an *azungu*, such as myself, whose experience of theological training is mostly derived from Western models, able to see clearly what may best be needed in quite a different cultural context. Even though our African lecturers have travelled to the West for their higher degrees, they will need to evolve models of formation that are more appropriate to Malawi than anything Westerners could dream up!

I know that the bishops had initially hoped that we might remain longer in Zomba so that I could initiate LKTC as its first Principal. But, while health and family considerations in any case now call us back to England, I am convinced that Malawi needs its own leaders at this stage of development. Sarah and I have very much appreciated our time here; the friendships and opportunities that we have so enjoyed will be etched for ever on our hearts and minds. We hope our contribution has been worthy of our UMCA forebears.

To all who have prayed for the work here to flourish, and have supported us with your letters and your gifts, our heartfelt thanks.

One final caveat: I am aware that many demands are made upon the generosity of your wallets, and there is a never-ending stream of appeals from worthy causes in Africa. Some of them are particularly heart-rending – and it is these that may need to be treated with caution, especially if they come from someone seeking help for school or college fees. Very few of these are likely to be genuine, and not all of them can be checked adequately from afar. The best way to be a 'partner-in-mission' is through a reliable Christian mission agency, whose grassroots contacts are in touch with the real needs and opportunities.

Please pray for the Anglican Church in Malawi, for the bishops, clergy and people – and especially for our ordinands and those who are as yet young in ministry.

POSTSCRIPT

Hoopoe
The hoopoe's cry is 'hoop-hoop' while offspring chirp 'sweet-sweet'.
Usually the crest is down, unless danger threatens.
The long beak is for probing the ground.

Trading from dugout canoes

When the Ilala drops anchor, it is besieged by dugout canoes. Passengers are assisted to embark or disembark with their katundu, goods are brought for sale, and spectators look on from the deck rail.

POINSETTIAS

LAKE MALAWI, geologically speaking, is a branch of East Africa's fault line known as the Rift Valley. This is the region where a number of fossil finds suggest that *homo sapiens* first evolved, before migrating further afield. I sometimes exploited this fact in discussion with politically minded students in Zomba who were prone to repeat the slogan 'Africa for the Africans'. I would rejoin with the observation that, in one sense, I too was an African – or at least had African roots. 'I daresay,' I would suggest, 'that many centuries ago one of my ancestors was a great friend of one of yours.' This remark was often greeted with incredulity, but the point was made that we actually belong to the same race living on the same planet.

Since those early days of migrating tribes, the world has shrunk considerably. In recent centuries trade and commerce have not only facilitated the exchange of resources and manufactured goods but have also opened windows on to other cultures, religious ideas and lifestyles. In particular, the Rift Valley which once exported the human race to other parts of the world is now able to import developments that have taken place elsewhere in the intervening centuries.

This may be illustrated by changes in Malawi's natural environment. Just as the Romans once introduced vines into Britain, and travellers abroad over many years (and especially in the 19th century) did the same with other exotic species, so too Malawi finds itself relying upon crops that were unknown not so long ago. Maize and tobacco, for example, are not native products, but like *poinsettias* and other colourful plants come from Central America. Yet if maize is regarded as a blessing, tobacco is now regarded differently – from which it is obvious that not all imported products (and beliefs) are equally desirable.

What then of the Christian faith, which is another late arrival on the scene? Perhaps an analogy can be drawn here with the way *poinsettias* seem to flourish in tropical Malawi compared with the potted versions that appears in Britain each year as cheerful Christmas decorations? When we first saw the vibrant red of *poinsettias* in our Zomba garden, and the height to which they grew, we could hardly believe it was the identical species. Yet it was indeed an African version of the same plant. Something similar can happen when Christianity is transplanted into a new environment. It can remain true to itself, while taking on more vibrant growth and native colour (even if elsewhere it may now be regarded as mere seasonal decoration!).

It is hard to predict with what local characteristics the churches in Malawi will continue to thrive. The diocese of Upper Shire has another bishop now in Brighton Malasa, last seen in these pages as a former student and then as a colleague at Magomero. Leonard Kamungu Theological College has been up and running for several years, with at least two former students involved in teaching there. When we were able to visit in 2008, we met in the chapel for worship together, and I was invited to give some account of the benefactions that had enabled the college to take shape. Yet, as anticipated, financing the work still remains a struggle and cash flow is erratic. Despite this, improvements continue to be made, and there is a good working relationship with Zomba Theological College, with whom some teaching is still shared. Sarah was particularly surprised – and delighted – to discover how well all her cuttings had taken, and how five years' growth had given the campus a mature setting.

The saddest outcome for the Anglican Church in Malawi happened eighteen months before our visit. Our friend Fr Rodney Hunter was the victim of poisoning and died by suffocation at the hands of 'a person or persons unknown' in his own house in Nkhokotakota. It is nevertheless quite clear that his death, after many years of devoted service in Malawi, was tied up with the disputes in the Lake Malawi diocese about the appointment of bishop Peter's successor.

Rodney's grave stone rightly records him as 'missionary, pastor and friend to the people of Malawi'. It was really because of his firm convictions that he was martyred. He was clear that it was worldly aspirations within his own diocese, even more than theological differences, which lay at the heart of the disagreement about the episcopal succession. His death did not, however, bring an end to the prevailing unpleasant atmosphere. Much more recently (in 2010), two of Rodney's young protegés were actually attacked in church in the presence of retired bishop Jack and a large congregation at an ordination service. They had to escape to avoid a severe beating – and the clergy present ignored what was happening, until the bishop intervened.

The divisive situation began much earlier when the previously mentioned American 'priest' Eugene Horn was in Malawi. His initial efforts to implant a 'born again' ethos met with little response, but when clergy found that there were financial benefits to be gained, unsurprisingly support started to come his way. He was given the backing of bishop Peter, who was initially unaware both of the extra incoming funds and of his irregular status and was therefore unsympathetic to Rodney's opposition. Before we left Malawi, Rodney had been suspended from his ministry as a result – but was reinstated the following year when the bishop discovered that monies had indeed been bypassing the diocesan office and that Horn's real intention was to create an African version of the Living Word Church (now known as the Bible Faith Fellowship) he had just founded in the States. Bishop Peter died soon after this, before he had time to mend the rift that had developed within his diocese.

When the see of Lake Malawi fell vacant, several clergy campaigned for an expatriate to be appointed from a London parish to succeed bishop Peter. The attraction was obvious: it lay, not in his pastoral experience or theological expertise, least of all in his familiarity with Malawi, but in his well-placed connections overseas whence money might be expected to flow into the diocese. Rodney's antagonism to such an appointment was compounded by the contender's evident liberal sympathies and careerist ambitions – but his real unhappiness was to see the old UMCA tradition of asceticism and simplicity of life, which he exemplified so well himself, being set apart by those who preferred Western models of affluence. To him, it was as if attempts were being made to uproot the plant he and others had nurtured over so many years, and to replace it with a noxious weed.

There is a phrase in English which describes those who are socially or financially motivated. They aspire to be 'upwardly mobile', and to achieve their goals can sometimes sit light to their inherited values and commitments. The Gospel, however, and the example of Jesus' own life are much more about the inversion of human values, to the extent that, if our eyes are directed towards God, they must surely also turn to look as he does upon those who are less successful, such as the poor and uneducated:

> You know the grace of our Lord Jesus Christ, that though he was rich, yet for your sake he became poor, so that by his poverty you might become rich.
> (2 Cor 8.9)

A real danger for some Christians in Malawi is now to ignore their lesser brothers and sisters at home, and to covet the greater prosperity of churches in the West. This individualism is not only a contradiction of the Gospel, but surely foreign to the 'communitarian' tradition God planted here long ago – a feature perhaps of what a 2nd century Christian writer called 'the spiritual Church founded before the sun and moon'.

Yet the continuing disturbances in the aftermath of Rodney's murder, and the reluctance of the Anglican Church of Malawi apparently to face up to the enormity of its occurrence, suggest that more is needed than fraternal respect. For life to flourish, for justice and peace, for the overcoming of bitterness and hatred, both penitence and pardon are essential. If anyone nowadays asks me what the Christian faith has to offer 'the warm heart of Africa', or if there is any point in being a missionary in the third millennium, my answer lies in the single word 'forgiveness'.

The four years we spent teaching and contributing to the well-being of Malawian people were worthwhile in themselves, although we certainly received so much more, in the richly varied experiences of friendship and community life, than we gave. But the *raison d'être* of our calling was truly the Cross of Christ, which must remain the measure of the Church's witness wherever it finds itself.

Whereas Charles Mackenzie mistakenly engaged in actual battle with passing slave traders, my real hero among the early missionaries, as must be quite evident, was William Percival Johnson. He was perceived by the Africans as a man of humility and moderation, who lived as he preached. His renown was confirmed by an incident that occurred one night in a village where he was staying. A lion was discovered prowling around, and was attacked repeatedly by men of the village armed with knives. None of them was apparently able to strike a death blow, and the lion continued moving threateningly between the huts. At last it reached Johnson's hut, and lay down at his door – and died without a further blow. Obviously it had been badly weakened already, but the villagers rightly saw this as the lion's recognition of Johnson's spiritual standing. Here was a man, perhaps a saint, who could call upon a greater power than the force of arms: it was God's compassionate strength exhibited in and through Johnson's life.

> Christians, listen to our Master
> teaching of the things above;
> Let our hearts beat firm and faster
> as he tells of God's great love:
> All are precious in his sight,
> our salvation his delight.
>
> Christians, see God's truth unfolding
> on the Cross before our eyes;
> There Christ suffers, still upholding
> faith and hope which man denies:
> We are precious in his sight,
> his compassion meets our plight.
>
> Christians, be renewed with Jesus
> in his resurrection power;
> Let his life and love now seize us,
> give us strength each testing hour:
> Jesus, precious in God's sight,
> share with us your glorious light.
>
> Christians, boldly now be willing
> to respond to God's design;
> Reaching out to need, and filling
> every place with joy divine:
> Lord, so precious in our sight,
> come among us with great might!
>
> **A mission hymn (RS)**

The mission hymn exhibits, I hope, that the Christian message of God's love and forgiveness is immensely liberating. As *The Times* columnist Matthew Parris, a declared atheist who happened to grow up in Nyasaland (as it was then) and who has revisited the country more than once in recent years, observed in a Christmas article of 2008:

Those who want Africa to walk tall amid 21st century global competition must not kid themselves that providing the material means or even the knowhow that accompanies what we call development will make the change. A whole belief system must first be supplanted. And I'm afraid it has to be supplanted by another. Removing Christian evangelism from the African equation may leave the continent at the mercy of a malign fusion of Nike, the witch doctor, the mobile phone and the machete.

On the basis of the evidence, Parris has changed his mind about the mission enterprise. He used to reckon that 'if faith was needed to motivate missionaries to help, then, fine; but what counted was the help, not the faith.' He now realises that 'this doesn't fit the facts. Faith does more than support the missionary; it is also transferred to his flock.' In his many dealings with Africans he found that 'the Christians were always different.'

> Far from having cowed or confined its converts, their faith appeared to have liberated and relaxed them. There was a liveliness, a curiosity, an engagement with the world – a directness in their dealings with others – that seemed to be missing in traditional African life. They stood tall.

Parris' account is of course a generalisation, but coming from a non-Christian it is a powerful testimony to the 'good news' which Christianity continues to offer Malawi, if only it is not confused with siren voices that promise effortless prosperity and rapid success. Maybe the vivid red of *poinsettias* is truly a reminder of the sacrificial cost of discipleship?

Black-eyed Bulbul
Every morning we woke up to his repeated call, 'Wake up Gregory ...'

MV Ilala
The weekly ship for passengers and cargo on Lake Malawi,
named after the village in Zambia where Livingstone died in 1873.

www.ingramcontent.com/pod-product-compliance
Lightning Source LLC
Chambersburg PA
CBHW050906300426
44111CB00010B/1409